A Modern Parable

Avalanche

The
9 Principles
for
Uncovering
True Wealth

Steve Sanduski | Ron Carson

KAPLAN

PUBLISHING

New York

This publication is designed to provide accurate and authoritative information in regard to the subject matter covered. It is sold with the understanding that the publisher is not engaged in rendering legal, accounting, or other professional service. If legal advice or other expert assistance is required, the services of a competent professional should be sought.

Vice President and Publisher: Maureen McMahon
Executive Editor: Jennifer Farthing
Acquisitions Editor: Shannon Berning
Production Editor: Karina Cueto
Production Designer: PBS & Associates
Cover Designer: Rod Hernandez

Published by Kaplan Publishing, a division of Kaplan, Inc.
1 Liberty Plaza, 24th Floor
New York, NY 10006

Printed in the United States of America

July 2007

07 08 09 10 9 8 7 6

ISBN-13: 978-1-4277-5467-7

Kaplan Publishing books are available at special quantity discounts to use for sales promotions, employee premiums, or educational purposes. Please email our Special Sales Department to order or for more information at kaplan-publishing@kaplan.com, or write to Kaplan Publishing, 1 Liberty Plaza, 24th Floor, New York, NY 10006.

"The best and most beautiful things in the world cannot be seen nor even touched, but just felt in the heart."

—*Helen Keller*

Also by
Steve Sanduski, MBA, CFP® &
Ron Carson, CFP®, CFS, ChFC

Tested in the Trenches: A 9-Step Plan for Building and Sustaining a Million-Dollar Financial Services Practice

PROLOGUE

I stood on top of the picnic table at my Aunt Kathryn's in Puyallup, just south of Seattle. I was goofing around with my cousin Jack, playing catch. Over his head, against a clear sky, I saw a mountain looming in the distance. It was a world away from my home in Chicago—a world away from the life I once knew.

I was only 18, but I had already lived two lives. Until two years ago, Dad had owned a large number of low-end rental properties, and he made a good income. We lived in a big house, took a yearly vacation to Florida, and owned a Cadillac DeVille. Mom took me on a big shopping spree down Michigan Avenue at the beginning of each school year, so I always dressed well. I was even one of the few kids in town to wear Puma shoes. The only downside was that Dad worked long hours, so he wasn't around as much as Mom and I would have liked. Playing catch with him was just an annual event. I could tell that his lack of time with me didn't make Mom happy. I pretended it didn't bother me.

One day, our lives changed forever. Dad walked into the house, and I saw fear on his face for the first time in my life. We were broke.

The domino that started it all was the sale of the bank that held Dad's rental property mortgages. The new owners felt that Dad had too much mortgage and personal debt, especially considering the recession. They quickly called in the loans. When Dad couldn't come up with the cash, he had to sell the properties at a fire-sale price. After paying off the loans, there was no money left. We had to sell the house and the Caddy and move into an apartment that Dad used to own. It was humiliating.

At 16, I was supposed to be driving and going out with girls. I had a date planned for that night, and suddenly it was off. All of my plans were off. Instead, I found myself holed up at home, alone, sitting on my beanbag chair listening to music. Music was my only relief from the embarrassment of living as if I was rich then losing it all due to my dad's financial blunder. The possibility of Dad losing all our money had never even crossed my mind.

Within a short time, though, everybody at school knew about it, and while some kids were still nice to me, others took cheap shots at my new status. "Hey poor boy," was a common insult I heard from these losers. They were always in a group, so I couldn't exactly punch 'em out.

Humiliation and embarrassment became a driving force in my last two years of high school. Because of these twin tormentors, I vowed that I would never be poor again and that after I got my college degree, I'd get a job where I could make a ton of money and live like a king again. King Andrew Craver, the First. Yes, I'd have the last laugh.

I wasn't the only one having trouble dealing with our new financial situation. Dad didn't take his mistake very well either. He tried to put on a happy face in front of me, but I knew he was a broken man inside. He kept saying, "We'll get through this," and, "I'll get it back," but he never seemed to believe it. Over time, he tried to numb his pain by turning to booze. That was his second mistake.

Mom and I wanted the family to move out of town and start over, but Dad refused. He said that would show weakness—that people would think he was a quitter and running away from his problems.

"I'm not a quitter, so get the thought of moving out of your head," he told us. "I'm gonna make a comeback. I'm gonna show those bankers they made a big mistake in pulling the plug on me." I desperately wanted to believe him.

For a year, he tried to get something going again in the real estate business, but nothing worked. He became a marked man in town. As his frustration grew, so did his drinking and his verbal abuse. Mom ended up taking a job so we could make ends meet, but that just made Dad even madder.

"I'm supposed to be the breadwinner in this family, not you," he screamed at her. Their relationship grew worse, and I was stuck in the middle of their cross fire.

About four months ago, on March 15, Dad finally threw in the towel. He said he was leaving town and heading to Florida—alone. He had some vague plan about selling real estate near where we used to vacation and he said he didn't need any additional baggage tagging along. Somehow Mom and I had been reduced to "baggage."

How could any Dad say something like that to his wife and kid? His words were so cruel, it was as though he had ripped out my heart and stomped on it. Mom tried to protect me, but she was dealing with her own pain. I heard her cry herself to sleep each night after Dad left. The day Dad left, I was so angry at him, I punched my fist through my bedroom wall. Leaving was his third mistake. That's when I stopped counting. He'd called a few times since he left to tell us what he's doing, but the calls were brief. Even my graduation a few weeks ago wasn't enough to bring him back.

When Aunt Kathryn called last month to congratulate me on graduating in the top 10 percent of my class and on being accepted to the University of Illinois, she invited Mom and me for a visit. Her timing couldn't have been more perfect.

Playing football with my cousin Jack was just what I needed—to feel like a kid again for one last time. I ran down the yard for a deep pass. Jack threw a tight spiral, and after I caught it, I spiked the football, did a little hot dogging, and yelled "Touchdown!"

Just then, I looked to the south and caught that incredible sight again—the ghost-white, glacier-covered Mount Rainier. It was so big, it practically blotted out the horizon. I looked at Jack and asked him if he had ever climbed it.

"Are you kidding?" he said. "I don't have a death wish. I don't think you'd want to climb it, either, if you knew how hard it was."

Looking back at the mountain, I smiled and took a mental picture.

CHAPTER 1

■

25 Years Later

In recent months, morning seemed to arrive before my body was ready for it. On one particular Thursday, it was a three-palmer; I had to hit the snooze button three times before I finally rolled out of bed at 6:20 A.M. Even then, I was still groggy.

Running late, I told my wife Sandra I didn't have time for breakfast. Instead, I stopped and picked up a doughnut and large coffee on my way to the office. Chicago's morning rush hour traffic can be brutal, so I figured the sugar and caffeine would help me stay alert. My boss, Leonard "Len" Wainwright, the demanding, irascible founder of Wainwright Development Company, wanted to meet at 8:30 to go over some final notes on a Wisconsin land deal before I headed up there later that morning to check out the property.

"This is the kind of deal I live for Andrew. It's big, it's bold, and it's going to be my legacy. I'm going to call the development Wainwright Shores," he said with his booming bravado. He wasn't kidding. As Len described it to me, this 61-acre piece of land was the prize of the Lake Michigan shore from Chicago all the way up to Sheboygan. Wooded, unspoiled, and situated on a bluff overlooking Lake Michigan, it was my job as Len's operational guy to do all the nitty-gritty work necessary to plop 40 multi-milliondollar homes in the middle of this pristine piece of property. Len was the "deal" guy, and I was the "detail" guy. For the most part, this complementary relationship had worked well over the past 20 years.

Len showed me a map of the property. He wanted me to go up there to walk the land and get a feel for it. He told me he had already talked to the owner, Edwin Luther, and convinced him that Wainwright Development Company was the right firm to buy and develop the land. The lawyers were in the process of working out the details. It wasn't unusual for Len to keep me in the dark this late into the game. He was a lone wolf who trusted his gut instincts, and he liked to wait until the last minute before he brought in his support team.

"There's a $1 million bonus in this for you once the land is developed and the 40 homes are sold," Len said, looking directly into my eyes. This was no joke. It was a big deal and I was going to deliver.

With those marching orders, I started out on my scouting expedition, heading up to the northern Milwaukee suburb in question. My red Porsche convertible hugged the road, and I turned up the CD player, playing dodgeball on the interstate. However, as I drove, my heart was heavy. It was the tenth anniversary of my father's needless death. Why did he choose to die as an alcoholic, alone and estranged from his family? It was a question I had asked myself often over the years.

Just past the Illinois border, as the traffic began to calm down, I thought about my dad and about how far I had come since the dark days of my last two years of high school. I remembered my vow that I would make as much money as

I could for as long as I could, so I would have the last laugh. Running through my mental scorecard, it looked good. I had the big house—check. Fancy vacations—check. Luxury cars—check. Another big bonus in the making—check. Every material thing I'd lost in my childhood was now back. Yet despite all these checkmarks, my reflection in the rearview mirror did not smile back.

Somewhere along the way, the incremental happiness I derived from moving up another rung on the ladder of success had started to recede. I realized I could only sleep in one house at a time, drive one car at a time, and take one vacation at a time. It wasn't supposed to turn out like this.

Reflecting on these life questions, I realized that I had no one to discuss them with. My single-minded financial focus left little time to cultivate one key aspect of happiness— meaningful relationships. Outside of my wife, my main buddy was Stan, a bachelor for life, fun-loving colleague who was not always a good influence on me. Otherwise, I had no fellowship community, no group of friends I could lean on and turn to during tough times.

Sandra said that over time, I had moved increasingly toward a state of what she called "emotional purgatory." I was absorbed with work, obsessed with money, and distant from her and our two kids, Kellie and Kevin. Neither she nor I knew what, if anything, was going to pull me out. And with Kellie away at college and Kevin busy with his junior year of high school, I wasn't exactly doing anything to get closer to them.

If Dad could see me now, he'd probably agree with the line from the Harry Chapin song, "Cat's in the Cradle." I had grown up to be just like him. Minus the alcohol, I had become my father's reincarnation—driven, money focused, and emotionally arid.

CHAPTER 2

I turned off the interstate and weaved my way through side roads. Nearing Edwin Luther's property, I saw a park and decided to pull in and walk inconspicuously over to the property from there.

The long and winding road that led to the Victory Park parking lot ended abruptly just a stone's throw from Lake Michigan. I stepped out of my head-turning car and saw the glorious lake, its rich blue hue providing a perfect backdrop to the swirling whitecaps. Despite having seen the lake literally hundreds of times from Door County down to Chicago and all the way up to Mackinac Island, it struck me differently that day.

I walked over to the bluff and stood there, soaking up the hot July sun, the sound of the seagulls, and the sight of the waves churning the sandy beach. As I inhaled the stiff breeze that carried a freshwater scent, an unusual feeling seized me. The problems I felt—the frayed relationship with Sandra, the detachment from the kids, the pressure of working for Len, pain-in-the-ass contractors—all those problems seemed to dissipate in that brief moment of serenity. I had no idea where this feeling came from.

Just as I was standing on that bluff feeling connected to life in a mystical sort of way, I heard a voice call out to me. Was it a dream? It was definitely a man's voice, and the tone suggested a very important and profound question. And then I registered it: "Hey buddy, can you throw that back to me?" I turned to see a stray frisbee at my feet, and suddenly I was delivered back to the present moment and my present problems.

Yes, I had a lucrative real estate career that enabled my family to enjoy all the finer things in life, yet I still had an indefinable ache. I was taking care of my family financially, but I wasn't taking care of them emotionally or spiritually. I wasn't making a difference in their lives or in society. I was asset rich but physically, emotionally, and spiritually broke.

While throwing the frisbee back, out of the corner of my eye, I saw a young couple canoodling on the bluff as they sat with their legs dangling over the cliff. Young and in love, that could have been me and Sandra 20 years earlier, but time and inattention on my part had frittered away our amorous feelings.

During the one-mile walk to Luther's property, a horrifying thought struck me. As my passion for my work and all its accoutrements grew, my relationship with Sandra waned. *Had I simply replaced my love for Sandra with my love for work?* The pain of that truth turned to anguish when I realized where Sandra and I could have been that day if only I had devoted as much attention to her as I had to my job. If only.

A split-rail fence marked the boundary of Luther's densely packed, old-growth forestland, and after looking both ways, I jumped it and ducked inside. As I headed east toward the water, I tried to picture streets, driveways, and homes coexisting with the magnificent, mature trees. I was awestruck by the immensity, the beauty, and the soul of the woods, and I had trouble figuring out how human intervention could improve upon what Mother Nature had taken an eon to create.

Len told me that Luther had a small cabin tucked neatly in the southeast corner of the land, so I tried to stay clear of it. Under normal circumstances, an agent would have given me a tour of the property instead of this somewhat discreet visit, but in this case, Len had worked directly with Luther. Since the deal was still in a delicate stage, Len did not want anything to get in the way.

"Try not to run into Luther while you're there," he said as I headed out of the office that morning. "I've got him right where I want him, and I don't want you to say anything to him that could possibly scuttle the deal." After I'd worked for Len for 20 years, he should have known me better than that.

After a leisurely 15 minutes, I reached the end of the path and stood gazing at the lake. In the distance, several sailboats lazily plied the waters. All work and no play, I had little time to enjoy my wealth, let alone sail in it.

"Hello." The sound of a man's voice startled me. "Muh name's Edwin Luther."

Uh oh, I thought, he caught me trespassing on his property. How am I going to wiggle my way out of this? Before I could regain my composure, Luther stuck his hands into his overalls and looked toward the water. "I often stand here myself; never get tired of the view and the sounds. Deer even eat out of my hands sometimes," he said.

I was relieved that he seemed friendly and in no mood to shoot me. "Do you live here?" I asked, trying to disguise my knowledge of the situation.

"For all my life, but not for much longer."

"What do you mean?"

"I have to sell the land and figure Ava and I will have to move somewhere else."

"Is Ava your wife?"

"For 42 years, God bless her."

Still nervous, I fumbled around for what to say. I blurted, "At least you'll make a killing."

He quickly set me straight. "No, no, I don't want to sell, and it's not about the money. It's about Ava. You see, she's been in and out of the hospital for some kind of infection that I don't understand. I never made much money but we got by, you know. Now with the medical bills, it's all we can do to keep from going under."

Edwin seemed saddened over the need to sell his land, and a part of me felt sorry for him. Without calculating the consequence, I said, "Have you considered selling just part of the land to raise the money you need for your wife, then continue living on the other part?" After I heard what I just said, I nearly choked. Here I was trying to squelch Len's deal and cut myself out of a big bonus. For the second time in about 30 minutes, an unusual emotion was sweeping over me.

"Well, you know, lots of people talked to me 'bout the land but not like you just said. They all tell me, 'You can be a rich man.' But they don't see that I'm already rich in what money can't buy. Most of 'em wanted to cut down the trees and build big houses. Then this man from Chicago comes up and says he loves the land, too, and doesn't want to cut down the trees. A Mr. Wainwright, I think he said his name was. Anyways, he says all he wants to do is build one building and use it as executive retreat. Don't know what executives need to retreat from, but he says he likes the woods and so do executives. He offered me much less money than the others, but I'm taking it because it preserves the land."

"Have you signed the deal yet to sell the land?" I asked.

"No, lawyers are talking. I don't know nothing 'bout contracts, just handshakes."

It was a classic Len strategy. Tell the seller what they want to hear and close the deal at any cost. To confirm my thought, I asked Edwin for clarification. "Let me make sure I understand this. You're selling the land because you need to raise money for your wife's medical bills, and you're selling it to a Mr. Wainwright from Chicago who said he's going to build an executive retreat and keep the land unspoiled?"

"Yep, Ava's sick and I got to take care of her. I don't want to sell, but Ava come first you know."

I wanted to know what would drive a man to leave so much money on the table, all in the name of preserving land, so I asked him to tell me why the land was so special to him.

"Come with me, but we gotta be quiet." He led me on a five-minute walk to a spot just a little farther inland. "See that?" he said, pointing up.

"Is that an eagle's nest?" I asked.

"Two of 'em moved here last year," he replied. "Paper says it's the first time eagles are nesting in southeastern Wisconsin since last century. We call 'em Abigail and Samuel and see 'em everyday."

Feeling a bit ashamed, I couldn't even remember the last time I saw an eagle.

"Eagles aren't the only good things here. Deer, fox, colorful birds . . . We don't need to go out—we got entertainment right here."

"How long have you owned this land?" I asked.

"Three generations. Over there, that's my house. Ava and me built it, mostly from logs on the land. Come in and we can have coffee. You seem like a nice enough fella."

Guilt began washing over me, and I decided it was time to go. I thanked him for the offer and politely excused myself. It was time to talk to Len.

I had about two hours to figure out what I was going to do. It struck me how some of life's most important decisions arise unexpectedly, with little time for contemplation. Would I follow the money and go along with Len's trickery, or would I stand up to Len and tell him I wanted no part of it—even if it meant forgoing my $1 million bonus?

CHAPTER 3

By the time I got to my car, the sky had turned cloudy, and the wind had whipped the water into an uncontrollable fury that relentlessly pummeled the shore. Was somebody trying to send me a message? I'm ashamed to say that when I turned the key to start the car, I honestly didn't know which Andrew Craver would show up in Len's office two hours later—the greenback chaser or the one that was beginning to want more from life.

Cruising on the highway, I was alone with my thoughts. Like the waves on the great lake, my mind swirled with conflicting emotions. *Take the money. Don't take the money. The Luthers will be fine. The Luthers will be devastated. Don't throw away a 20-year career. I can reinvent myself. What would Sandra think? What would the kids think? Can I look in the mirror and smile?*

I reached back into my memory and thought about the early days of my career. Coming off my dad's problems, I was passionate about making it big in the real estate business. In some noble way, I felt a duty to make up for the inglorious way his career ended. Yes, I admit I wanted to make some serious cash, too, but my intentions were honest. And they stayed honest . . . for a while.

Greed has an insidious way of sneaking up on you.

Early in my career, Len took me under his wing, and my first few deals with him were clean. I was enjoying the ride and my income, and my bank account grew steadily. I remember thinking if I could just make a guaranteed $100,000 a year, then I'd be set for life. Once I hit that goal, however, my bogie rose to $150,000 . . . then to $200,000 . . . and it kept rising. Looking back, I can see that I was on a slippery slope—as my income grew, so did my appetite for more.

Len sensed that I was enjoying my growing net worth and gradually, he helped me cut corners. I began shaving a little here and greasing a hand there. All I knew was, nobody seemed to be getting hurt, and I seemed to be getting richer.

Over time, as the shaving and greasing grew, I started to make little deals with myself. I found intellectual ways to justify my transgressions. However, I discovered that you could tell your mind one thing, but if your heart knows the truth, then your body will rebel.

I easily could have blamed Len for my sinking integrity, but that would have been a cop-out. The fact is I made my choices. I acquiesced.

Outside of the office, my relationship with Sandra had its own trajectory. Back in the early days, we didn't have a lot of money, but like the mythical Waltons, we worked hard, lived on love, and were very happy. Now that I had a lot more money and worked just as hard if not harder, I had less love and only fleeting happiness. Somewhere along the way, my formula for a successful life developed a greedy crack, and it split my relationship with Sandra and the kids.

Needing some advice, I hit the speed dial on my cell phone and called Stan. I'd met Stan Devlin my senior year in college, and we both ended up working in the real estate business in Chicago. He was an agent at a rival company, but we became fast friends who shared a passion to indulge in life's hedonistic pleasures. We were both wild and single in the early days. In fact, he still is. When Sandra and I got married, he was my best man.

Over the years, Stan had been sort of a free shrink for me. Someone I could talk to, man-to-man, about guy issues, family, and the occasional insecurity. I'd often wondered though, what does it say about me when I'm taking advice from a middle-aged, party-mode bachelor whose prized possession is a 1997 Lamborghini Diablo? Despite this concern, I shared my dilemma with him on the drive to Chicago that afternoon, and he had a novel way to reduce my cognitive dissonance. He said I should keep quiet, develop the property, then give away some of my profits to worthy causes— enough to relieve my conscience. I gave him an A for creativity, thanked him, and then hung up.

Ultimately, I had to make the decision.

CHAPTER 4

Slowly, I eased my car into my reserved parking spot and turned off the ignition. I headed up to Len's office and shut the door. I looked him straight in the eyes and spoke slowly and deliberately so there would be no misinterpretation. "Now tell me exactly how you got this deal with Mr. Luther?"

Len calmly said, "Sit down," as he motioned to the leather couch. He collected himself and tried to put on his fatherly demeanor. I think he sensed that I may have learned some of the details of the deal and that I was not happy about it. Len was an expert at adapting to any situation, and he could be comfortable mixing it up at a black-tie fund-raiser or up to his neck in mud, checking on a new development. He had a short temper honed over the years by dealing with a myriad of contractors and suppliers who never seemed to do things to his satisfaction. At 6'5" and 260 pounds, he was also very intimidating.

"Here's the deal," he said. "Edwin Luther needs money to pay some medical bills, and he decided to sell his land to raise the funds. I caught wind of the situation and paid him a visit. When I realized his love of the land, I told him we could keep the land relatively intact by building an executive retreat center and still give him a fair price."

"Len, come on, you know that's not what we plan to do. You told me you wanted to build 40 houses on that land."

"Andrew," he said, "We both know that if I told Edwin what we really planned to do with the land, he would never sell it to us at this low price. Look at it this way; Edwin gets the money he needs to take care of his wife, and we get a great property to develop. Nobody gets hurt."

"Except Edwin. I know because I unintentionally ran into him on my visit today. You're toying with a man's heart and soul here. He loves that land, he loves his wife, and you're lying to him to grab it away below market price."

Len's gaze was unwavering. "Andrew, they're just old trees with a nice lake view, so don't get too worked up about it. We'll cut down a few trees, build some great houses, and move on. The Luthers will have more money than they'll ever need, and Mrs. Luther will get her medical bills paid. Where's the harm? We sign the deal in a couple weeks, and you're my man on this. With that million-dollar bonus, you'll have plenty of money to soothe your conscience."

"Look Len, I know we haven't always been on the up-and-up in past deals, but this one feels different. *I* feel different. I saw in his eyes what that land means to him, and I'm having trouble taking it away from him. Can't we do something different here?"

"Andrew, we've worked together for a long time, and you know this business is cutthroat. If we don't do this deal, some other developer will step in and say what they have to say to get Edwin to sign. He's going to get shafted either way, so why not by us? I'll tell you what, if it makes you feel better, I'll tell Edwin that our company will chip in up to $10,000 to help defray his wife's medical expenses. That's fair."

It was a classic negotiating technique. Len threw me a $10,000 bone to satisfy my need to justify this transaction.

There was an awkward silence in the room as Len looked down and I looked up. I thought that was indicative of our source of guidance. Len couldn't believe that I was having trouble going along with the ruse, and I couldn't believe he was so blatantly lying to close a big deal. My heart rate had to be pushing 160 beats a minute as beads of sweat started rolling off my face.

"Len, for years I've slowly compromised my integrity, and while I won the mansion, I lost my soul. But no more. It's time for me to move on and rid myself of the toxins in my body. Today is the day I raise my standards. I quit."

"Quit? You can't quit, Andrew. What's gotten into you? I'm handing you the biggest deal of your life, and you tell me you're quitting? I plucked you out of college more than 20 years ago and made you a millionaire, and now you can't just walk away right before I'm about to close my most important deal. If it's the money, I'll give you more money. Just don't quit on me like this."

Len's face reddened with anger, and his chest puffed up. I decided to leave before we came to blows. He just couldn't understand that I had reached my limit. I couldn't keep living the way I was living. I really wanted to quit. I *had* to quit.

I walked out of Len's office and went to my car. Drained, I slumped over the steering wheel with my head in my arms and started crying uncontrollably as all my emotions from the past and present came pouring out. Dad's financial failure. My parents' divorce. My own failure as a husband and a father. And now this, quitting my job. What was I thinking? A 20-year-plus career—gone. A mid-six-figure income—gone. The identity I'd wrapped myself in since college—gone. Was I stupid? For just one more chink in my moral armor, I could have been on my way to soothing the pain by cashing a $1 million check. Instead, I was rehearsing how I was going to break the bad news to Sandra.

CHAPTER 5

■

As I pulled into the driveway of our home late that afternoon, I noticed the stately oak trees that served as an enduring sign that this was no ordinary home. It was big. At 9,600 square feet, it stood out even among the other giants of the neighborhood. It was weathered but in a good way, and the home exuded wealth, stature, and prestige. Situated in a gated community, it was perfect for entertaining—and showing off—which I did frequently. By living in the home, I felt as though I had finally arrived. All the hard work and sacrifices had paid off, and I had finally made it to "the party."

I walked into the house and saw Sandra standing at the top of the stairs. For a moment, we just locked eyes. I remember thinking how beautiful she was when I first met her, with her flowing hair, her confidence, and her style. She was always opinionated and had strong convictions about religion, money, family, and love. I'd found that very attractive.

After years of an obsessive pursuit of business success, I had lost sight of what I so loved in her, but in that moment, as our souls met across the stairs, there was a flicker of that old chemistry. I believe Sandra felt it, too, but she could sense something was out of kilter with the universe. Women have this way of looking in your eyes and reading a story without words. My story that afternoon was short and sweet: *I quit my job.*

I started to explain the whole situation to her, hoping that my reason for quitting would soften the blow of my having put our family's standard of living into serious jeopardy. I was totally unprepared for her reaction.

She looked at me and said she couldn't believe what I did. Sobbing, she threw her arms around my neck. I thought she was going to choke me. After a few seconds, I grabbed the sides of her upper arms and pushed her back. Looking at her eye to eye, I told her I was sorry and that I'd find another good-paying job so we could still maintain our high lifestyle.

Between her tears, she said, "You don't get it do you?" I must have had a dumb look on my face. "See these," she said as she took my left hand and wiped the tears from her eyes. "These aren't tears of anger; these are tears of hope. You made a lot of money from this job, but it also turned you into someone I couldn't live with." She took a deep breath then said, "Now we have a chance again."

CHAPTER 6 ■

As I tossed and turned in bed that first night after quitting, the full moon entered my line of sight through the south-facing dormer window. Just as the sun's light illuminates the moon, so too did the moon's light illuminate Sandra. I laid on my side and just looked at her. Peaceful, graceful, and timeless—just looking at her as she lay sleeping had a soothing effect on me.

The next morning, I got up and ate breakfast with my son. He knew something was up, because I rarely ate breakfast with him. I turned to him and in all seriousness said, "Kevin, you need to be aware of something. I quit my job yesterday. It's a long story, but your mom and I both feel good about the decision. I don't know what I'm going to do next, but we'll get through it."

"I'm sorry to hear that, Dad. Can you pass the milk?"

Can you pass the milk? Boy did that hit me like a ton of bricks. I just quit my job of 20-plus years, and all my son could say was, "Can you pass the milk?" It dawned on me just how far removed I was from his life.

Unemployment was unsettling. My predictable daily routine and my reason for getting out of bed were gone. For years, I had lived to work. It fed my ego. It paid the bills. It was my identity. Without work, I'd essentially lost my purpose in life—shallow as it was.

Life doesn't always smack you on the side of the head and tell you what to do next. I knew my short-term goal was to figure out how to save Edwin's property from development yet still get him the money he needed for medical bills. But after that, then what? Fortunately, I had an idea for Edwin's problem, and I spent the first three hours that morning researching it online.

Satisfied that I had a workable idea, I drove back to Wisconsin early that afternoon, and unannounced, I knocked on Edwin's door.

"Oh, back again, uh, Mr. Craver, right?" he said.

"Yes, and I'm sorry to bother you, but I really need to talk to you." I was nervous, not knowing how he would respond. He kindly invited me inside for the coffee I didn't have time for the day before.

The Luther home was definitely early American, as in lots of wood and not a lot of conveniences. Termites would have felt right at home.

I told Edwin that I had to confess something. As I paused briefly to try to find the right words, he filled the gap and said, "I'm not a priest you know, but if it make you feel better, I listen." We both chuckled and that eased some of my apprehension. Edwin's simple view of life was refreshing.

Finally, I summoned up the courage to tell him what was going on. "I came here yesterday at the request of Mr. Wainwright, the guy who told you he wanted to build an executive retreat on your land. My goal was to look at the land and start getting an idea of how we could build 40 multimillion dollar homes here. There was no plan to build an executive retreat. We planned to tear down a lot of the trees, put in roads, and make this an exclusive subdivision."

In the few seconds it took me to confess, Edwin's demeanor completely changed. From the genial German an instant ago, Edwin now looked like a beaten heavyweight boxer sitting on a stool, arms draped over the ropes, and unable to answer the bell for the 15th round. He blinked rapidly to prevent the water in his eyes from turning into tears that, nonetheless, streaked down his cheeks. I realized change could indeed happen in an instant.

"But how could you?" asked Edwin, drained of his life energy and barely able to muster a response.

In a repentant tone, I said, "I couldn't, and that's why I'm back again. Before I came to your land yesterday, I viewed it as one more conquest in a long string of conquests. One more subdivision to build and bonus check to cash. Then something happened. Walking the land, feeling the life here, meeting you and hearing your story, it hit me. I still can't explain it, but there's something real about this place and about you and Ava that made me realize I can't come in here and tear it up. And the fact that Mr. Wainwright lied to you to get you to sell the land cheaply to him . . . Well, I just couldn't do that."

Edwin was completely at a loss for words, so I kept talking.

"I want to help you. Actually, I need to help you. I have a plan that can save the land and get you the money you need to take care of Ava. We can put an easement on your property and sell part of your land to a land trust. Then you can live here for the rest of your life. By selling to the land trust, you'll have the money you need to pay for Ava's medical bills."

Edwin began to perk up. "Why would you do this for me? Is it for money?" he asked.

"I'm doing this because for once in my life, I'm going to do the right thing. And no, I don't make money from this. My payment comes from seeing you live on the land and helping you get the money you need for Ava." I was beginning to see that not everything in life should be measured monetarily.

A grateful, but still somewhat skeptical Edwin said, "What about that fella from Chicago? He thinks we got a deal." Edwin had a good point. Len would explode when he heard about this.

"Let me take care of him," I said, not knowing exactly how I was going to do that.

"Okay, but you better hurry. I'm nervous about all this," said Edwin. He reached out his hand. We shook and sealed the deal. Fortunately, I didn't have a noncompete agreement in place with Len, so he couldn't sue me for interfering with his deal.

Once I got back to Chicago, I didn't waste any time. Over the next few days, I did more research and started calling attorneys and conservation organizations to try to make this deal happen. Two conservation organizations expressed an early interest and said they would start their due diligence process.

It didn't take long for Len to find out what I was doing. In fact, it only took about 24 hours before he called. "Andrew, you traitor, how could you do this to me?" he yelled over the phone. "I made you a lot of money, and you repay me by trying to cut me out of this deal?" I'd expected the call and had thought carefully about how I would handle it.

I told him I appreciated what he'd done for me over the years, but I just couldn't bear to see how Edwin was being treated and I was just trying to make the situation right.

Then he stabbed me with his words, asking, "Since when did you get a conscience? Money has always meant more to you than anything else. Even if you didn't like what I was doing, why didn't you just leave the deal alone? You made your point by quitting; you don't need to compound it by screwing up my deal. I just can't believe you're doing this to me after all I've done for you. I've treated you like a son."

I could understand where he was coming from, and I told him I was sorry, but what was acceptable to me in the past was just no longer tolerable. I was raising my standards. He wasn't buying it.

"We'll see how long that lasts. You love money and the lifestyle it buys just as much as I do. You'll be back." Then he slammed the phone in my ear.

That phrase, "You love money," ricocheted in my head. He had me pegged. For 20-plus years, it *had been* all about the money.

CHAPTER 7

Mom had a hand in honing my competitive drive. I remember telling her when I was just 12 years old that I wanted to be the absolute best at something. At the time, I was a good all-around athlete, but I wasn't great at anything. She told me there were three things I had to do to become the absolute best at something:

1. I had to find something I loved.
2. I had to practice it consistently and deliberately.
3. I had to keep it up for ten years.

"Success isn't sudden, and neither is failure," she used to say.

Oh how I miss her at times like this. When she died three years ago, a part of me went with her. After Dad left, she was all I had . . . until Sandra came along. When she lay dying, she confessed that Dad didn't choose to leave the family—she kicked him out because of his verbal abuse and alcohol. For all those years, I'd thought that Dad had completely abandoned us, but that was only partially true. Since Mom's death, I've often wondered how differently his life—and our lives—might have been had they been able to work things out. I'll never know.

By the time I met Sandra, I was already hard at work in my real estate career. I loved the business and it showed. Most of my waking hours were devoted to it. Unfortunately over time, that put a strain on the rest of my life.

From outward appearances, Sandra and I had a great life. We had two kids who were healthy, bright, and likeable; a stately home; and, up until I quit Wainwright, a great-paying job. I had reached my major goal in life, which was to make a lot of money. Sandra, whose needs were nonmonetary, had good friends, two kids who depended on her, and a full schedule of helping at school, serving in the community, and playing tennis to stay fit. But like many things in life, looks can be deceiving.

I was overweight, and my diet was as clogged with junk food as my veins were with cholesterol. Prior to quitting my job, I came home from work cranky, and by the time I unwound from the stress, it was time for bed. I made little time for Sandra and the kids. Financially, I earned an excellent income while working at Wainwright, but our savings, while good, should have been higher given our cash flow. Over the years, numerous financial advisors had contacted me, but I'd ignored them. I followed my own financial plan, which was essentially to pay the bills as they came due and not overdraw the checking account. Despite my obsession with money, I put image first and future security last.

They say opposites attract, and that was true with Sandra and me. She grew up in a family that cherished humility and gratitude, while I was all about "living large," as the kids say these days. The family finances also concerned her, but despite her protests, I went ahead and put our family's savings plan on hold by buying "the house with the stately oaks" a few years ago. Something had to give, and I didn't know if we could bend without breaking.

With no job and no income, money began flying out of our bank account. Mortgage payments, car payments, the gardener, the maid, tuition payments, credit card bills—it all piled up. I suddenly had a flashback to the day Dad walked in the house and told Mom about the bank's calling in his loans. I now understood how he must have felt—feeling like a failure for not protecting the family's financial resources. As a man, I wanted to be the provider; I wanted to be the rock. Instead, I felt like a fraud.

Aside from helping the Luthers, I had time on my hands in the first few days after I quit. For someone who was used to hard work and long hours, hanging out at the house was rather depressing. I had time to think about my life and what I wanted to do, but there were no easy answers. Should I stay in real estate? Should I do something completely different? Was I really a financial failure? How could I let my family down like this? Was I having a midlife crisis? I didn't know, and the scary fact was, I had no idea how to go about finding the answers. This whole concept of self-reflection was foreign to me. Ever since I was 16, I'd known exactly what I wanted to do, but now, for the first time in more than 25 years, I had to come up with a new plan.

With the right attitude, it could have been a great situation. I was talented and smart and had a lot going for me. Instead, I let negative thoughts overwhelm me. I became depressed and more detached from Sandra and the kids.

I soon discovered, though, that everything in life is connected—frequently in ways we never expect.

We had an old couch in the basement, and about two weeks after I quit my job, as Sandra tried to make me useful, I moved it. Thinking I was still 25, I manhandled it and wrenched my back. Bent over and in pain, I realized that my youth and health had escaped my body while I was busy chasing status symbols with about as much substance as a jellyfish.

Unemployed and now hobbled—this wasn't exactly how I pictured my 40s.

CHAPTER 8

Stiff as a surfboard, I paid Dr. Graham a visit the next day.

Dr. Graham had been my doctor ever since I was 27. He was only 12 years older than me but clearly much wiser. During the visit, I explained my back pain, and he asked if anything else was hurting besides my lower back.

"My ego," I said somewhat offhandedly, knowing he didn't have a pump to inflate it.

"Ego," he said in a tone that invited a response.

"That's right. It's a long story, but the bottom line is, I quit my job a couple weeks ago, and now I'm lost. For more than 20 years, I was a workaholic, and my job defined me. With work came money, prestige, perks, and accomplishment. Now it's like 'no job, no self.'"

Doctor Graham knew me pretty well. He could tell that in addition to my physical pain, my spirit was broken. "How long has this been brewing?" he asked.

"For about the past two or three years, I've been feeling a general malaise. I'm even hitting the snooze button more often, whereas in the past, I didn't even set the alarm because I just woke up naturally."

"Hitting the snooze button is like having cancer on your enthusiasm," he said.

"I suppose the snooze button was a symptom of other problems, too. I'm irritable, my work wasn't satisfying anymore, I'm not connected to the kids, and Sandra . . . gosh I wonder why she still puts up with me. That's probably more than you want to hear, isn't it?"

Surprisingly, he said, "Andrew, your sore back may turn out to be fortuitous. I can help you with the back pain, but it's the pain in your spirit that I'm more concerned about."

"So what do we do?" I asked, almost rhetorically.

"We've got some heavy lifting to do, but first, let's take some X rays. Then on your way out, stop at the front desk and tell Angela that you need to set up an aerial meeting with me."

"What's an 'aerial meeting'?"

"Andrew, you've trusted your health to me for a long time. Now I need you to trust your well-being to me, too. The aerial meeting is the first step. Now let's get that X ray taken."

Dr. Graham was average height with a lean, solid build; his physical presence was not overpowering. I wouldn't classify him as your ordinary doctor. When he spoke, his eyes seemed to say as much as his measured and reassuring words. His hands were warm and comforting, and he had an air about him that was as discernable as it was indefinable. Being a general practitioner for 20 years, "the good doctor," as I overheard some of his patients call him, had to be financially successful, yet by material possession standards, you would never have known it. I noticed that he drove a functional car and lived in a modest, middle-class neighborhood. And rather than being a workaholic, he worked only on Tuesdays, Wednesdays, and Thursdays, a schedule he started early in his career. I thought that was a little curious, because he could have made a lot more money if he worked a full week. He never married, but he'd mentioned that he and his brother were close.

The X rays came out okay, and my discs were fine. The only problem was my spine, which was a little out of alignment. Dr. Graham said a few adjustments, cardiovascular exercises, and strength training would take care of the problem. After getting my commitment that I would follow the prescribed exercises, he asked me a strange question. He asked if I had ever climbed a mountain, and I told him no, except for some hikes in Arizona.

He said, "When you stand on a mountain, you see things from a new perspective because you're on a different plane." He went on to say that my back pain would go away soon but my other pain would take time to heal. And for my other pain to heal, we would have to go on a trek, which would require me to look at things from a new mind-set. "Are you with me?"

At that moment, I realized that life presents just a handful of turning points, the kind that can alter your path forever. Going away to college, getting married, having children, taking a new job, quitting a job, and the death of a loved one are a few of them. Dr. Graham's keen interest and sincere tone made me believe this could be one of those turning points, too.

I trusted him, so I said, "Yes."

CHAPTER 9

■

On the drive home, I wondered what I had just committed myself to. Was I really ready to step out of my neat and tidy comfort zone?

Thirsty, I made my way to the kitchen and grabbed a glass of water. Just then, Sandra came around the corner and to my surprise, put her arms around me and gave me a hug. "What was that for?" I asked.

"I'm your wife; do I have to have a reason to hug you?"

"Good point." After the brief but pleasant embrace, I told her that I'd seen Dr. Graham and that his advice to me was to do some heavy lifting.

"Heavy lifting? Isn't that the last thing you need to do with your sore back?" she asked.

"He didn't mean *that* kind of heavy lifting. He could tell just by looking at me that my spirit seemed broken. He said my back would be fine after I do some exercises but the rest of me will take some time to heal. I didn't realize it was that obvious."

Sandra's expression changed from neutral to hopeful. "So did he tell you what he meant by 'heavy lifting'?" she said gingerly.

"Not exactly. He said the next step was for me to come back and have a meeting with him; he called it an 'aerial meeting.'"

"What's an aerial meeting?"

"I don't know. I asked Dr. Graham what it was, and he said I just needed to trust him and that I should set up the appointment with Angela, his receptionist. So on my way out of the office, I asked Angela, and she gave me this warm smile and said it's nothing to worry about, that it's actually a good thing if I'm receptive, and if I keep an open mind. We set the meeting for 1:00 P.M. next Thursday. Then she gave me this envelope and asked me to read it when I was ready."

"What did she mean by, 'when you're ready'?"

"I have no idea. She was really vague about it. She just said it was from Dr. Graham and that it was very important that I review it."

"Well, are you ready to open it now?"

"Not right now, but maybe later." I tried to brush it off for a while. Part of my problem was that I was good at avoiding things that might make me uneasy. Sandra knew that, but she wouldn't give up. She wanted a specific time. "Kevin's going to the youth group meeting tonight, so we'll have some time alone. Why don't we plan to open the envelope after he leaves? This could be good for us."

Although I tried not to show it, Dr. Graham's mysterious envelope had piqued my curiosity. Frankly, I was in no position to argue. Unemployed, lost, and out of shape, what did I have to lose? Dr. Graham was a well-respected doctor, and I had known him for years. If anybody could help me, he seemed like the guy.

Sandra's prodding was what I needed. "All right, let's open it later tonight."

That evening, we passed around Dr. Graham's envelope and fiddled with it like two nervous teenagers. It was as if we both knew this envelope could hold the key to something special.

"Go ahead, open it," said Sandra, not wanting me to delay the suspense any longer.

Just as I was about to reach into the envelope to pull out whatever was in there, I looked at Sandra and said, "Are you sure you want me to read this?"

"Yes, yes!" she said, looking happy that I was being a bit playful.

Inside was a neatly folded piece of Dr. Graham's stationery. It didn't take long to read. I turned to Sandra and said, "You'd better read this."

I didn't know what to expect, but I certainly didn't expect this.

Be a living example of . . .
Stick to . . .
Be driven by . . .
Be accountable through . . .
Cherish your . . .
Value your . . .
Wisely use your . . .
Find ways to . . .
Be open to . . .

It was just a piece of paper with several incomplete sentences. That's it. No instructions, nothing else. I told Sandra, "If he's trying to help me, why didn't he finish the sentences instead of making me guess?"

"I think he's telling you that these are questions you have to answer on your own, through your own discovery process."

"He's the doctor, not me. I'm paying him to give me answers, not to go on wild goose chases."

"Andrew, listen to you. These aren't easy issues we're dealing with, and you're already dismissing Dr. Graham."

"I don't want to talk about it anymore. I just hope my meeting with Dr. Graham next week is not a waste of time like opening up this letter was. I'm gonna go to the study and read."

"Wait. There are other things we can talk about. Kevin won't be back for a while, and we should take advantage of our time alone."

"Like what other things?"

"Us," she said passionately. "Honey, remember when we got married? We talked about how there were going to be good times and bad times and that during the bad times, we couldn't bail. I know times are tough now. You're out of a job, your back hurts, and we're not as close as we could be. But don't give up. I'm so proud of you for how you stood up for your convictions regarding the land deal. That's the Andrew Craver I married. We can get through this and be stronger for it."

"Thanks for the vote of confidence, but I don't feel very talkative right now. That letter was a waste, I have a big house with no job, and my first priority is to get back to work. Right now, all I want is a drink. I'll be in the study."

As I walked away, I could feel Sandra's eyes on my back and the weight of her disappointment.

CHAPTER 10

◼

"Dr. Graham will see you now." The nurse's calm voice did little to reduce my uneasiness as I walked into Dr. Graham's office for the aerial meeting.

"How are you?" he asked.

"Well, honestly, I've been better," I said in a rather hushed tone.

"I'm not a big fan of doctors' offices, so why don't we grab a cup of coffee and then go for a walk out back," said Dr. Graham. How ironic, I thought, a doctor that doesn't like doctors' offices.

As I took my first sip of coffee, I noticed that Dr. Graham skipped the coffee and instead made hot tea. "Not a coffee drinker, huh?"

"No, I switched from coffee to green tea back in medical school, but I still enjoy the aroma of coffee. Have you ever noticed, Andrew, how certain aromas can naturally put you in a relaxed state of mind?"

"Well, I've been so tightly wound up the last few years that I really haven't paid much attention to my sense of smell."

"When was the last time you went for a walk in the woods?" he asked.

"It's been awhile. Probably about 10 years. Back when the kids were younger, we used to go camping once or twice a year with some friends, and we always had a good time being outdoors and milling around the campfire."

"Then you're overdue. Let's head out back."

When Dr. Graham had located his office here years ago, people thought he was nuts. Who in their right mind would locate a doctor's office out in the middle of nowhere? It would be generous to say that his office was on the edge of town. It was more like he was in his own town. Yet despite the remoteness, his practice thrived, and his patients never hesitated to make the long trek. Amidst 80 acres of burr oaks, red maples, and evergreen trees, the setting was inspiring and very untraditional. Then again, so was Dr. Graham.

"Last week you were as down as I've ever seen you, Andrew. I could see in your eyes that something was troubling you."

"Yeah, as I said last week, I quit my job, and I've been irritable, cranky, and at a loss for how to move forward. My back hurts, I'm overweight, my relationship with my family is on the rocks, and I'm concerned about my finances now that I'm unemployed. I'm just a mess, doc." With no close friends to confide in (Stan wasn't able to grasp what I was going through), this was the closest I had come to really opening up to another human being. For some reason, I felt comfortable around Dr. Graham, and opening up to him in this way was rather therapeutic.

"You're not alone, Andrew. Everyone experiences pain at points in their lives. Think of pain as weakness leaving the body; it's only bad when we wallow in it and use it as an excuse to mope around and do nothing. I know from the success you've had in the past that you are not the type to let a temporary setback turn into a permanent one."

"But this setback feels different. It's not something that just happened. Instead, it's been building. I've had this uneasy feeling that my life is just not in sync the way it should be. What's confusing about this is, on the surface, I'm living the American dream. Everything I own is big. I should be pinching myself. Instead, I'm punching myself."

"Perhaps the American dream is not something you own. It's something you are."

"You're probably right. I'm finding that even though I have great material wealth, I'm not much happier than when I was poor and just starting out."

"Did you forget anything in your definition of the American dream, Andrew?" Dr. Graham paused and looked straight at me, as if he was trying to communicate telepathically.

"Oh yeah, my family. We're not so hot right now, so I guess it wasn't exactly at the top of my mind. Man, I'm really a schmuck, aren't I?"

"As odd as this may sound, Andrew, you've already taken a big first step. Ah, perfect timing. Let's dispense with the talk for a moment. We have a decision to make. The trail ends here and picks up on the other side of the stream. Unless you want to get wet, the way to cross it is to grab that rope and swing."

I looked at Dr. Graham as if he were crazy. Why would two grown men swing on a rope in the middle of a forest? Good thing there was no candid camera around.

Without hesitating, Dr. Graham went first and made a clean landing on the other side. He tossed the rope back to me. There was no way I was going to let a 50-something, gray-haired guy show me up on an athletic challenge.

When I put my full weight on the rope, the tree branch holding it bent noticeably. The way my luck was going, I wouldn't have been surprised if it snapped and I ended up taking an unintended bath. After a few harrowing seconds, it held, and I made it across. A minor rope burn and an elevated heart rate were the price I had to pay to keep up with my fit doctor.

As we continued walking, Dr. Graham commented, "You've added a few pounds over the years."

"A few? More like 35, and most of it is concentrated in my gut. I was so busy at work and stressed out that I never found time to work out or watch what I ate. Now I'm paying the price." Dr. Graham had an uncanny way of getting me to open up without even asking a question. Just a mere comment about something was enough to start my mouth.

"The sad thing is, back in high school and college, I was in great shape. That fell by the wayside once I started working. Now I'm one of the millions of Americans who are overweight and underexercised. Being unemployed and with time on my hands, I should probably start exercising, so my time on the dole is not totally useless."

After another half-hour of conversation, we came upon the stream again.

"Okay doctor, how are we going to get across this time?"

"Well, like many things in life, you can take the easy way or the hard way. Let's follow this path for a moment."

After rounding the bend, the easy way came into view. "A bridge, how convenient. Why didn't you tell me earlier that there was a bridge? Then I wouldn't have had to risk my life on that swing."

"Andrew, we always have options. Sometimes we just have to look a little harder."

"All right. Let's do something a little crazy here." Rather than take the bridge, I decided to jump in the stream and wade through. Prepared for anything, Dr. Graham was right behind me. About halfway through, I stopped and completely submerged myself. "If I'm going to get wet, I might as well get completely wet," I told him.

By the time I reached the other side, I felt rejuvenated.

"I'm happy to see you didn't want to take the easy way back, Andrew. That attitude will help you immensely as you start your exercise program to lose those 35 pounds."

I figured Dr. Graham must have taken a sales class. His "assumptive close" on the exercise program was smooth and effective.

"This little walk today was invigorating. I haven't been out in the woods in years, and I don't think I've ever played Tarzan like that. Maybe Sandra would like to play Jane . . ."

"That's a little more information than I need to know, Andrew."

"Just kidding. Seriously, I do want to lose these extra 35 pounds. That little rope swing gave me a rush of adrenaline and made me realize just how sedentary I've become."

"It's easy to lose sight of the importance of taking care of our bodies. When we get back to the office, stop at the front desk and tell Angela you need to contact Tamara Ross. She's a personal trainer who can help you develop a new lifestyle plan. By working with Tamara, you'll rediscover how having excellent physical health will promote excellent mental health. It will also help you deal with the loss of your job and the resulting effect on your finances."

"Thanks, I'll call her later today."

Dr. Graham put his hand on my shoulder, a man-to-man gesture that belied our growing friendship, and said in a hushed tone, "That's a wise decision."

Fortunately, it was a very warm day. As we walked back to the office, the sun took care of drying out our clothes.

"You mentioned finances. That's another area I need to figure out. When I was working and earning a big paycheck, I didn't really worry about money. We bought whatever we wanted, and as long as there was money in the checking account, things were fine. But now, with no job and no income, my lack of planning is coming back to bite me. Sandra is frustrated with me, because she has been telling me all along that we needed to save more money and not live so large. I hate to admit it, but she was right. I guess I never thought I'd quit my job."

"Andrew, sometimes the most important lessons in life have to be experienced, not taught."

"Well, I'm experiencing this one. Got any bright ideas on how I can get my finances back on track?"

"Just like you sought out me to help heal your body, you need to find a competent and trustworthy advisor to help you financially."

"Do you know anyone like that?"

"I do. As you can imagine, as a doctor, financial advisors contact me frequently. I've met with a few of them over the years and developed a good feel for how they operate. What I've discovered is, there are several types of advisors. Depending on your needs, any one of them might be a fit. In your case, with your net worth and your sophisticated needs, I'd suggest you work with a wealth advisor. Wealth advisors look at your entire financial situation and develop a plan that considers your tax, insurance, and estate planning needs in addition to your investment goals."

"If I'm going to share all that personal stuff with someone besides Sandra, I'm going to need to totally trust them. Who would you recommend?"

"Hank Kinnick. He and his staff take the time to get to know their clients' hopes, dreams, and aspirations and then systematically work toward achieving them. He's helped me achieve mine."

"Sounds like a great fit, but I sense a 'but' coming."

"You're getting perceptive, Andrew. He is very popular, but his first priority is taking care of his existing clients. That means he only accepts a handful of new clients each year."

"Do you think he would work with me?"

"Possibly. He only works with people whom he thinks he can truly help, and more importantly, who want to be helped. Just let him know that I referred you. You can get his contact information from Angela before you leave today. And if you do work with him, don't forget to involve Sandra. Finance is a family affair."

As we neared the end of our walk in the woods, I felt refreshed rather than tired. Getting some fresh air, swinging on the rope, and opening up to Dr. Graham had helped lift some of the fog that had enveloped me.

"Andrew, this is a very special time in your life. You can use the adversity you face as a catalyst for future growth, or you can wallow in self-pity. I'm here to help you in any way I can."

I considered myself a rugged individualist, and I was not used to leaning on others for help. However, Dr. Graham seemed to have the right mix of old-world wisdom and modern-day understanding that I needed.

"You've already been a big help. I'll call the trainer and the advisor and meet with them. I'll also keep doing the back exercises you gave me last week. And before I forget, I have one question. You called this an 'aerial' meeting. What the heck does that mean?"

"*Aerial* is just a form of the word *air*. It simply means that we are going to meet outside. I find that walking through the woods, especially when you pay attention, is a great way to clear the mind and open the senses."

It had worked: I was already starting to feel better.

CHAPTER 11

It was strange waking up each morning with no place to go, no sense of urgency, and no destination driving me. Years of hard charging had conditioned me to a fast-paced, never-a-minute-to-spare morning routine that was now wildly out of kilter. Instead of rushing to get out the door, I could take my time. Ironically, the stress-free mornings were stressing me out.

Looking for a job was not yet on my radar. After the gut-wrenching decision to quit, I just couldn't drag myself to look through the want ads or network with friends. It was still too raw. On the other hand, I was shocked to learn that our savings dwindled by an average of $1,000 for each day I convalesced. Financially speaking, the Rolling Stones had it wrong; time was not exactly on my side. So contacting Hank Kinnick was a high priority. Maybe he could help me figure out how to make our savings last longer.

Hank's office sent us an information kit that we had to review before we could set up the planning meeting. The cover letter asked Sandra and me to complete a "Confidential Profile," which contained numerous questions about our goals, objectives, and appetite for risk. We had to complete the forms separately, and as we compared notes, it appeared that

I was more of a risk taker, while Sandra was more conservative. No surprise there.

Because we were thinking about our finances, I decided to do a back-of-the-envelope calculation of our net worth, something I hadn't done for a while. I added up all our assets, including our house, other real estate, our investments, and our money market fund, then subtracted our outstanding loans. The number was certainly well above the average family's net worth but less than I was expecting. Frustrated, I looked at Sandra and complained about how little I had to show for more than 20 years of hard work. She quickly set me straight.

"Andrew, your self worth does not equal your net worth. Don't forget, we have two kids who are doing great, and we have reasonably good health. I think we're millionaires in those departments."

"I know, but those departments don't pay the bills." Worrying about paying the bills was a new and uncomfortable feeling for me.

With an increasing sense of urgency, I dropped the packet in the mail the next day, and Hank's office responded quickly. His assistant Jane called to set up an appointment for the following week.

CHAPTER 12

Two days later, I met with Tamara, the personal trainer recommended by Dr. Graham.

As I pulled into the parking lot of Feelin' Fit, an aerobics, nutrition, and fitness center, doubts started to creep into my head about whether I really wanted to shuck my sedentary habits for the stair-climber and the bench press. Working hard on the job was easy, but working out—that was a different proposition altogether. Just as my negative self-talk was reaching its peak, an Arnold Schwarzenegger look-alike walked out of the gym, closely followed by a glistening woman in spandex. That was it. That was the signal I needed.

Once inside Feelin' Fit, I liked what I saw and heard. Tony, the general manager, greeted me with an enthusiastic smile and a firm handshake. "Welcome to Feelin' Fit," he said, "How can we help you?"

"I'm new here, and I have an appointment with Tamara Ross. Is she available?"

"That's her right over there in the brown outfit." He pointed to a woman who stood out even from 50 feet away. "I'll take you over there."

As we reached Tamara, I realized why she stood out. A striking brunette with long hair neatly wrapped in a ponytail, she had a sculpted figure and a welcoming smile.

"Andrew, I'd like you to meet Tamara. Tamara, this is Andrew."

With the formalities out of the way, Tony departed.

"It's so nice to meet you, Andrew. To get started, let's go to my office and talk about a few things."

As we sat down, Tamara picked up her notepad.

"I'm so glad, Andrew, that you have decided to focus on your health. What I'd like to do is ask you a few questions so I can get to know you a little better. From there, I can outline how we will proceed. So for starters, can you share some of your life story with me?"

"Well, I grew up just outside of Chicago and went to the University of Illinois. After college, I took a job with a real estate firm here in Chicago. I stayed there for over 20 years and made a lot of money, but I paid the price by working long hours, eating poorly, and neglecting my wife, Sandra, and our two kids. A few weeks ago, a situation at work arose, and when push came to shove, I ended up quitting over it. My whole self-image was wrapped up in my job, and now that's gone. I met with my doctor, Dr. Graham, because of a back problem, but he could tell I had problems that went beyond the physical. As part of my 'recovery,' he knew I had to work on my physical fitness, and he referred me to you. So here I am. I'm sorry for rambling; that's probably more than you wanted to know, isn't it?"

I was concerned that I had opened up too much to this woman who was a total stranger just five minutes earlier.

"Oh no, Andrew, thank you for sharing," she said as she compassionately reached out and touched my arm. "So much of physical fitness is mental fitness. Stress at work or home can greatly affect your physical fitness. The more I know about your environment and where you are coming from, the better job I can do of helping you become physically whole. How's your stress level now that you are not working?"

"It's a different kind of stress. When I was working, I had the pressure of a demanding boss, incompetent contractors, and always trying to finish the job ahead of schedule and under budget. That pressure's gone, but now I have the stress of paying bills with no income to pay them. We have a decent savings cushion, but I feel like we're committing a sin by dipping into principle. So yes, stress is my daily companion."

"How have you dealt with stress in the past?" she asked.

"By eating and isolating myself when I get home from the office. Not real effective, huh?"

"There are better ways," said Tamara with a knowing smile. "Okay, before we go any further, let's take a moment and try to destress. I want you to close your eyes, relax all your muscles, put your hands on your thighs, and just breathe. Focus on your breath. Breathe deeply and exhale completely. Now let's do that for a couple minutes."

I felt funny sitting there with my eyes closed and doing nothing but breathing. My mind began to wander, and I tensed up. After a minute, I couldn't take it anymore.

"This feels weird. I'm tenser now than I was before the breathing exercise. If this is how you work, then maybe this isn't such a good fit."

"I understand your apprehension. Let me tell you something about me, Andrew. Years ago, a sports injury made me very bitter. To help get things under control, I visited a doctor, and the first thing he did was pour me a cup of green tea. That was fine, but he kept pouring until the cup overflowed. I yelled at him to stop, because the cup was full and it was spilling all over the carpet.

"He looked at me and said, 'Tamara, like this cup, you are full of anger, and we can't get anywhere until you empty yourself of it. When you are empty, we can start filling it with peace.' I thought it was weird, too, but I gave him the benefit of the doubt, because he was an experienced doctor. I'm glad I did, because over time, I was able to overcome my anger and replace it with a calm understanding. I just ask that you give me the same benefit of the doubt."

"That story sounds pretty Zen to me," I said.

"You can call it what you want, Andrew; the label is not important. What I'm going to ask you to do is step out of your comfort zone and go to a place you've never been before. To prepare for this physical plan, you need to rid yourself of your bad habits and limiting beliefs. So let's continue; I have a few more questions. Were you physically active in your younger days?"

"Actually, I was very active. In high school and college, I did a lot of bike riding. Just riding out in the country for miles and miles—it was sort of my way of getting away from things. You should try it sometime. But after college, work took over and the riding faded away. I've been pretty inactive since."

"It sounds like you know what it's like to work hard, sweat, and get in the zone."

"Oh yeah," I said proudly if not a bit pompously.

"How about your eating habits?"

"They're about as good as my exercise habits. I'm also a sucker for chocolate, especially 3 Musketeers® bars and M&M's®."

"I can see we've got some things to work on there," said Tamara, as she dutifully took notes.

"I've got a question for you, Tamara. When it comes to being physically fit, which is more important, eating right or exercising?"

"That's a great question. As a personal trainer, I'm going to tell you both are critically important. It's really about balance. The nice thing about eating healthy is, we have to eat, so making better eating choices won't take any more time out of your day. Exercise, on the other hand, does take time but not in the way you think. You'll spend more time exercising, but you'll have more energy during the day, so you can get more done. As they say in the business world, your 'productivity' will increase."

Looking for an easy way out, I asked, "If I can lose weight just by eating better, what if I just focus on my diet and skip the exercise?"

"Then you'd need a new trainer," she said. "When you hire me, you get the complete package. Diet and exercise are two of my core values, and I see it as my mission to help people get on the path toward holistic wellness. You may not value these things today, but as we work together and you start to feel better, you'll come to understand why I am so strong in my belief."

Her conviction was coming through loud and clear to me.

"Tell me more about you. How did you become a personal trainer?"

"Thank you for asking, Andrew. As a 5'10" high school sophomore, the coaches said I should try out for volleyball or basketball. I tried volleyball, and it worked out well. I ended up going to college here in Chicago. But in my senior year, I blew out my knee, and that ended my career. Consequently, instead of playing, I became a student trainer under the direction of our team doctor, who was very inspiring to me. As you may have guessed, our team doctor was Dr. Graham—that's how we met. I liked the training and helping other people so much that I made it my career, and Dr. Graham has been my mentor."

"So Dr. Graham was the green tea doctor. That Zen story sounded like something he'd do."

"Yes, he's wonderful, and he's been a big influence on me. He helped me put my blown-out knee in perspective. Andrew, why don't you tell me about your objectives? What are you hoping to accomplish by working with me?"

I noticed how Tamara deftly found a way to turn the focus back to me and away from her.

"One thing I want to do is lose weight. I had a great visit with Dr. Graham the other day, and he inspired me to focus on my health. That's why I called you."

"Thank you for sharing that. I'd like to get more specific here. Let's take a few measurements so we can get a baseline, and then we can track your progress. If you would, please take your shoes off and stand straight against the wall. Five feet, eleven inches. Now the scale. Two hundred ten. Now your waist. Forty-four inches. All right. I also like to do a body fat measurement. These are skin fold calipers and I'm just going to take a few pinches. And don't worry—they won't hurt. And how old are you, Andrew?"

"Forty-three," I said, slightly embarrassed that this taut woman was finding big patches of flab to pinch with her overgrown, scissor-like calipers.

"According to the chart, your body fat is 28 percent," she said matter-of-factly.

"How bad is that?" I asked, unfamiliar with the concept of body fat measurements.

"According to the American Council on Exercise, anything over 25 percent is considered obese for men."

"Obese?" I said, loudly.

"You're not alone, Andrew. Nearly two-thirds of our population is overweight or obese. It can sneak up on you."

"Yeah, it snuck up on me right here," as I took both hands and jiggled my gut. "I'm really pathetic."

"You're not pathetic at all. You've just been under a lot of stress and your diet was poor, but you can change that. If you make the commitment and are willing to put in the effort, I can help you get close to that lean cyclist you were back in college. I'm not saying it will be easy, but I'd like to be your health coach along the trek. You need to trust me. Are you with me?"

Those words sounded familiar, because Dr. Graham had used almost the same wording when I met with him after I hurt my back. He'd taught her well. Tamara seemed to have a paradoxical charm about her. She was clearly a taskmaster when it came to getting fit, yet she conveyed a sense of concern and genuineness that made me feel comfortable.

"Before I say yes, what am I committing myself to? I want to get in shape, but I don't want to kill myself in the process."

"Andrew, if you don't get in shape, you will kill yourself. I don't mean to be dramatic, but carrying those extra pounds, particularly around your midsection, puts you at a much higher risk for diabetes and heart disease. Rather than focus on the negative, let's think about your future for a moment. Imagine it's one year from now. You've lost 35 pounds. You can run five miles in 40 minutes, and you take 25-mile bike rides with your kids just for fun. You get by on six hours of sleep and still wake up refreshed without an alarm clock. After your early morning workout, you eat a healthy breakfast topped off with a nutritious fruit smoothie. Several small meals throughout the day keep your body fueled. Your energy level is on par with Jack La Lanne in his prime. Your pulse is down to 50 beats per minute, because your heart is strong and pumping a large volume of blood with each stroke. Sandra comments on your stamina and how sexy you look. Is that worth some extra effort?"

"Were you ever in sales, Tamara?"

"No, why?"

"Because you just sold me big time. I'm in."

Pleased with that response, Tamara proposed a workout schedule that included meeting on Monday, Wednesday, and Friday for weight lifting with solo cardio workouts on Tuesday, Thursday, and Saturday. Sunday would be a day of rest.

She also asked me to track my food intake for two weeks so she could see how well I was eating. After a walk-through of the weight-lifting equipment and filling out some paperwork, we were done for the day.

CHAPTER 13

Hank's cover letter made it clear that he expected us to come prepared for our first meeting. I grabbed a folder and stuffed our tax return in it along with a recent brokerage statement. He already had our "Confidential Profile," because we had to mail it back before he'd set up the meeting with us.

As Sandra and I walked off the elevator to Hank's office and turned to our right, we met Jane. As ebullient in person as over the phone, she immediately made us feel welcome and at home when we walked in. Soft music, mood lighting, a menu, and unusual magazines, like *motto,* rounded out the experience of the first 30 seconds.

"Mr. and Mrs. Craver, it's so nice to have you here with us today," said Jane ever so politely. She engaged us in a good six minutes of conversation before Hank appeared.

"Good afternoon, Mr. and Mrs. Craver," said Hank, "I've been looking forward to meeting you. Let's go have a seat in my office."

As we walked into Hank's office, you could sense this was a man in charge. He was tall and muscular with a confident and reassuring style about him. The way he carried himself suggested this was a man moving on purpose.

After some small talk, he got down to business. "So tell me about you."

Not missing an opportunity to turn the spotlight on myself, I proceeded to replay my life story over the next 10 minutes—despite the occasional stomped foot I received under the table from Sandra. I think my blatant grandstanding embarrassed her.

An experienced advisor, Hank skillfully handled the situation. Not one to have the spotlight on him, he asked us a series of questions to help him further understand who we were and where we wanted to go. We did most of the talking, and Hank seemed to be a good listener.

After about an hour, Sandra decided it was time to turn the tables and find out more about him. "Hank, can you tell us about you and your firm? What makes you different from other advisors?"

"That's a great question. While there are many advisors you could work with, I think we're doing something very special here. It really started about 40 years ago. My father passed away unexpectedly when I was 10, and he left us with a small amount of insurance and little savings. I had a front-row seat as I watched my mother struggle to work full-time and raise three kids. While money was tight, the love wasn't. Somehow, we made it, and my mom remarried and lived a full and happy life. The experience left an indelible mark on me. It gave me the desire and conviction to work with families to help them grow their assets and achieve financial peace of mind. I want to help other people avoid the struggle my family went through, and I want to help people protect what they already have. That's our mission, to help people achieve financial peace of mind. My passion for helping families grow their wealth and protect their assets from the unforeseen, borne out of my experience of growing up after my dad died unexpectedly, is what makes our firm unique."

"Is that a true story?" I asked. Before Hank could answer, Sandra jabbed me with a stiff elbow to express her displeasure at my disrespect.

"Yes it is. We're really passionate about what we do here because I've seen firsthand what can happen when proper planning is absent," said Hank, seemingly unperturbed by the question.

"Well, I know we haven't done proper planning," said Sandra.

"Unfortunately, many other people haven't done so, either. I have a good feel for your situation now, and I'm confident we can help you. The next step is for us to create a wealth plan, which we can discuss at the next meeting. If the wealth plan developed by our enhanced services team addresses your hopes, dreams, and aspirations, is there any reason why you would not move forward with our firm?"

"I don't see why not," said Sandra.

"Wait a minute. I don't even know what this will cost us. Surely you don't do this for free," I said.

"A portion of our business is pro bono, but that is reserved for those who would have difficulty paying for advice. You're fortunate to be well off, so yes, we do receive compensation for our services." Hank then explained the compensation structure.

"So the next step is to review the wealth plan at the next meeting?" asked Sandra.

"That's correct. If the wealth plan meets your needs, we'll have you come back to authorize the paperwork, and we'll start the proactive wealth-management process. As soon as the assets arrive, we'll invest them according to our agreed-upon plan. From that point forward, you'll hear from us on a very regular basis, and we'll continue to monitor and adjust your plan as appropriate."

"That sounds good to me," said Sandra.

"I'd like to wait until I see the wealth plan before making any commitments. This is my money we're talking about, and I don't want anything to happen to it," I said.

"I can appreciate that, Andrew. Managing other people's money is a tremendous responsibility that we take very seriously, and we try to take care of it with as much respect and sound judgment as we do with our own money. Just so I understand where you're coming from, Andrew, if we put a wealth plan together that meets all your needs, is there any reason why you would not move forward and implement the plan with us?"

"Well, if I can trust you and if you do what you say you're going to do, then yes, I suppose we'd move forward." I was a little hesitant, because that meant I'd have to give up managing our money myself. But then again, I wasn't doing so hot on my own, and Hank did come highly recommended from Dr. Graham.

"Andrew and Sandra, I do have one final request for you. Normally, I'd wait until you became clients, but I think in your situation, it makes sense to ask you now. Part of my personal mission is to help people, not just financially, but also personally. I'd like you to go to my website, *www.truewealthcommunity.com,* and download a booklet that I call "Blueprinting™." Blueprinting attempts to help people like you answer some of life's big questions. Please take some time to go through it. I promise you will find it enriching."

"Blueprinting, huh?" I said, as if taunting Hank to explain it more thoroughly. He took the bait.

"Blueprinting is a process of self-discovery. Through a series of thought-provoking questions, you'll listen to what your heart tells you and end up with a clarity for your life that will bring you added meaning and purpose."

"Sounds too touchy-feely for me. I thought you were a financial advisor, not a shrink."

Before Hank could respond, Sandra interjected, "I think a little sensitivity training would do you some good, Andrew."

"I understand your concern, Andrew. Men tend to be a little less open to the Blueprinting process. Women, on the other hand, tend to embrace the idea of self-reflection and spending time thinking about life's big issues. However, if you take it seriously, Andrew, it will change your life."

"We'll see," I said.

After some additional small talk, we set a time for the next appointment, shook hands, and headed out.

On the way home, Sandra expressed her displeasure at my behavior with Hank. "I can't believe how boastful and disrespectful you acted in there. What's gotten into you?"

"I know I was a little out of line, but talking about money reminded me of how I'm not making any right now. I guess I used this as an opportunity to talk about myself and pump myself up a little bit. It was my ego talking."

"Honey, I know you're down because of the work situation, but that's just temporary. Lean on me instead of lashing out. Let me be your rock for a while."

Sandra was reversing the roles on me. I thought I had to be the strong one because I'm a man, but Sandra seemed determined to do whatever was necessary to keep me on the right path.

"When we get home, let's download the Blueprinting packet. Maybe it can help us," she said.

"Not tonight. I'm not in the mood to think deeply, but we'll look at it soon."

"Are you afraid of something?" she asked.

"You just don't give up do you? But if you must know, yeah, I'm a little scared. I'm scared of what I might find. I'm scared of examining my life and coming up short. Arrgh, I just want to scream."

"Don't worry, honey, I understand."

Sandra then curled her hand in mine and gave me one of those glances that needed no words. Twenty-one years of marriage had produced a language not found in any linguistics book.

The rest of the ride home was rather silent except for the sound of the Beatles *Abbey Road* CD wafting through the speakers. I could relate. There was something in the way Sandra moved . . .

CHAPTER 14

A couple of days after the meeting with Hank, I was finally mentally ready to get serious about the Blueprinting Exercises. To get started, I downloaded two sets of the exercises from Hank's website at *www.truewealthcommunity.com*. To set a mood, I unplugged the telephones and started playing a long CD of the mesmerizing sound of waves crashing against the shore. The only things missing were candles and incense.

We sat on the floor and got comfortable as Sandra read the instructions. "It says that Blueprinting is a series of five exercises that will ask you to reflect deeply on your life and think consciously about how you want to live it. By living your life by design, not by default, you will gain a new clarity that will profoundly impact you, personally and professionally."

"Hank's not mincing any words there, is he?" I said. "So what are these five exercises?"

Sandra read them off.

1. Values clarification
2. Finding your meaningful purpose in life
3. Creating a compelling vision for your future
4. Creating a personal mission statement
5. Setting goals

"Is that all? We'll be done in half an hour," I said sarcastically.

"Andrew, let's take this seriously. These look like good questions, which might help you finally open up to me. Here's a piece of paper. For the values clarification exercise, all you have to do is write down your six most important values in order of priority. I'll do the same, and then we'll compare our lists and see how similar they are."

Values Clarification

1. _____

2. _____

3. _____

4. _____

5. _____

6. _____

As we started writing down our values, the sun escaped from the clouds and cast a beam of light into the family room. The illumination, coupled with the sound of waves crashing on the shore, created a soothing ambiance that relaxed me.

"Let me know when you're done," said Sandra. It didn't take her long to complete her list, because she was already in tune with the important things in life.

"Okay, what do you have?" I asked.

"I've got faith at the top of my list, followed by family, financial security, friends, concern for others, and health."

"Looks like we overlap. I have family, self-reliance, faith, wealth, achievement, and knowledge on my list."

"You've got family at the top of your list," said Sandra in a disbelieving tone. "Do you really think you live as if your family is your highest priority?"

"You just said to list my highest values in order of priority. You didn't ask me to list them in the order that I was following them. So yeah, I probably don't live as if my family is most important. But I do things like work hard and earn a good living so our family will have money to live in a nice house, go to good schools, and basically have every advantage to succeed."

"Andrew, when are you going to learn? The kids and I would have gladly traded your long hours and hard work for more of you. If you really want to live as if we are your most important value, then forget the money. Material goods are no substitute for your time, attention, and your love."

Deep down, I knew I worked hard because I enjoyed the high from business success and cashing bonus checks. Sandra knew it, too.

"Well, I'm unemployed, so you've got my time."

"I don't mean just your time. You need to be fully present with us. Sitting in the same room with us reading the newspaper doesn't count as giving us your time. Interact with the kids. If you really want to turn me on, show some interest in this family. Initiate a game of H-O-R-S-E with Kevin, or help Kellie with her career planning. Seeing you enjoying time with them makes me feel close to you. And if you really want to score points, clean up the kitchen after dinner and load the dishwasher without my asking."

"It's that easy, huh?"

"Love is not rocket science, but I want you to do these things because it brings you joy, not because you think it's going to lead to the bedroom."

"I get the idea. What's next?"

"Hold on. You said you have self-reliance second on your list. You need to realize that you're part of a family—our immediate family, an extended family, a church family, and a family of friends. Rely on us. Don't just rely on yourself."

Sandra's comments were starting to get too preachy for me, and I was about to wave the white flag before we even finished the first exercise.

"Look, Sandra, I'm not perfect. I'm just telling you where I'm at now. Maybe I'll change. As time goes on, I'll mature, my priorities will change, and I'll be a better person."

"And I want to be a part of that. I don't mean to preach, but this is a chance for us to be open with each other. The more you can share with me, the better."

"Fine. Can we move on now?" I said rather testily.

"I don't think this is going to get any easier. The next question is, 'What is your meaningful purpose in life?'"

What Is Your Meaningful Purpose in Life?

1. _____

2. _____

3. _____

4. _____

5. _____

6. _____

"I have no idea what my purpose is. I know my motivation to be successful came from my childhood, but I don't think just making money is a worthy purpose."

"No, but doing something constructive with money could be," said Sandra. "Is there anything in our community or in society that touches you, that moves you to take action?"

"Do you remember a couple of years ago when that downtown apartment fire left 40 families homeless? I was the one who suggested we donate money to the Gimme Shelter Fund."

"And that's good, but I don't think writing a check when a tragedy happens really qualifies as a life purpose. Think about what really burns inside of you. What can you do that uses all your skills, interests, talents? What do you feel like you were put on this earth to do?"

"Well, when I was younger I wanted to be a rock star. Does that count?" I asked half-jokingly.

"Not unless you're Bono. He's using his music and his celebrity to go out and make a difference in the world."

"Yeah," I said, feeling rather small by comparison, "I'm no Bono."

"Your purpose in life doesn't have to be as grand as Bono's. For me, I think raising good kids is a grand purpose. We can't all be Gandhi, so we shouldn't beat ourselves up over it. What we can be are people who make a difference. We're still young and have lots of life ahead of us. When Kevin's out of the house, we'll be in an even better position to contribute to society."

"Good point. However, I still don't know what my purpose is."

"Just being aware that we are all here for a reason is a start. Keep thinking about it and be open and attentive to the signs around you. Your purpose will eventually come to you."

"Man, you're good at this. How'd you get so smart?"

"I'm a woman."

"And just the kind I like—smart, sassy, and good looking."

After pausing for a moment, I had a thought. "You know, there is one thing that I'm becoming more passionate about. Do you remember last summer when Kellie dragged me to the bookstore to hear that author talk about climate change?"

Sandra nodded in encouragement.

"He was very convincing, and since then, I've been thinking about this whole global-warming thing. He talked about all the glaciers melting and what a disaster that could be."

"What are you thinking?"

"Well, if there is some truth to global warming, then I'd be interested in doing something about it."

"Like what?"

"I'd want to do something that uses my real estate background, so maybe something in the residential solar energy business. I haven't researched it yet, but on the surface, it seems like a good industry to be in, and it would help the environment."

"What, you'd manufacture solar energy panels?" asked Sandra.

"Probably not manufacturing, because that would be capital intensive. I was thinking more along the lines of being a distributor and installer of residential systems."

"That has possibilities, but you're not exactly mechanically inclined. I have trouble getting you to change a furnace filter."

"I would hire someone to do that part. My role would be to start the business and generate sales. It's just an idea now, and I'd have to do a lot more research. I'll spend some time on the Internet and maybe make a few phone calls and see where it leads. Anyway, what's next on our exercise list?"

I was starting to feel encouraged by the process.

"The third item is to create your compelling vision of the future, a written narrative that describes your ideal life. It includes things like what you do, whom you surround yourself with, where you live, and what your purpose is."

"How long of a narrative?" I asked.

"It doesn't say, but the example in the booklet is a few paragraphs long. I'll read it to you, but it's written from the standpoint of a man."

As Sandra read the sample compelling vision, I thought to myself that I'd like to have that kind of life, too. It was definitely compelling. "How are you supposed to get started on writing something like that?" I asked.

"Here, it lists a few questions to get you started."

Create a Compelling Vision of the Future

1. What is your ideal working environment, including your location and surroundings?

2. Who are the people you want around you?

3. What type of work do you want to do?

4. If you had 26 hours in a day instead of 24, what would you do with those extra 2 hours?

5. If you only had only six weeks to live, what are the six most important things you would want to do before you die?

6. If money was not an issue, what would you spend the rest of your life doing?

7. What makes you feel alive and energetic?

8. What community or world issue could prompt
   you to take action?

9. What aches inside of you?

"This is going to take some time," I said. "I'm going to get some coffee. Do you want some?"

"Yes, honey, and thank you for asking," said Sandra, with some extra enthusiasm in her voice. It was rare for me to get the coffee, and Sandra seemed to appreciate the gesture.

"You know, Andrew, rather than each of us having a separate vision for our future, why don't we just create a single vision for our family? That makes more sense to me than each of us doing our own separate thing don't you think?"

"I think you're right, but I'm still drawing a blank on how to get some initial words down on paper."

"Try this idea, but don't take it as an omen. Start writing your eulogy. Go to the end of your life and pretend you're looking backward. What do you want people to say at your eulogy?"

At first, the idea of writing my eulogy sounded morbid. However, once I started writing it, it was helpful. After a considerable time and through playful back-and-forth, Sandra and I created a draft of our compelling family vision.

"Andrew, this has been so good. I really like what we have here."

"It feels good to me, too."

"Is that a tear in your eye?"

"No, just a speck of dust that caused my eyes to water." Even though I'd cried my eyes out after quitting my job, I still wasn't very good at dealing with emotions, but I was starting to feel them that day.

"The next thing we need to do is create a personal mission statement," said Sandra.

What Is Your Personal Mission Statement?

1. _____

2. _____

3. _____

4. _____

5. _____

6. _____

"How does that differ from the vision we just created?"

"It looks like the vision is more of a big-picture, long-term view of what you want your life to be like, whereas the mission is more of a day-to-day road map and decision-making guide. In the instructions, it equates the mission to the route you take up a mountain, while the vision is what you see when you are standing on top. It also says the mission should be short enough that you can remember it."

"I can see why it makes sense to have one vision for the two of us, but for the personal mission statement, it seems like we should have separate ones. Our day-to-day activities and roles are different enough that having our own personal missions is probably a good idea. What do you think, honey?" I asked.

"That makes sense," she said.

The ocean waves CD had already looped a couple times, so Sandra got up and changed it. She searched our neatly organized archives and found a George Winston CD. It was just the right sound to keep the emotions flowing and provide an excellent backdrop for relationship building.

"This personal mission statement is so hard to write," I said. "Trying to be brief is not easy."

We each shared the draft of our mission statements. Sandra's was succinct at just three sentences, yet it still touched on several areas. My mission statement was a little longer, and as a nod to my business personality, it contained several bullet points.

"It's definitely neat and orderly," said Sandra. "I can see how you could use it as a guide to make daily decisions. Now we have to keep refining them and make sure we live the way we write."

We were making great progress, with four down and one to go. "Why don't you give me the packet, and I'll lead us through the last exercise," I said. "I'm already good at goal setting. We have, or should I say 'had,' to set goals every year at work, so this should be no problem."

Family Goals

1. _____

2. _____

3. _____

4. _____

5. _____

Personal Goals

1. _____

2. _____

3. _____

4. _____

5. _____

Business Goals

1. _____

2. _____

3. _____

4. _____

5. _____

I started to take charge, and Sandra was happy to see me so engaged. "I haven't seen you this excited since the Bulls won their sixth NBA championship," she said.

"That was awesome, wasn't it? Okay, time for goal setting. It says your goals have to meet the 'SMAC test.' SMAC stands for specific, measurable, achievable, and compatible.

- By *specific,* it means your goals have to be clear in terms of the desired outcome.

- *Measurable* means your goals have to be quantifiable, leaving no gray area as to whether or not you've achieved them.
- *Achievable* means that when you set the goal, you should set it in such a way that you think you have about a 50–50 probability of achieving it.
- And *compatible* means your goals have to be in harmony with your values, meaningful purpose, and mission."

"Does it mention any categories for the goals you set or what time frames you should use?" asked Sandra.

"It says you should set family goals, personal goals, and business goals and then break them into 1-year, 5-year, 10-year, and 20-year goals. Geez, that's a lot of goals. Why don't we just start with 1-year goals and then set the family goals together and set the personal goals individually. And then I'll set some business goals since I'm the only one working, or at least planning to work."

"That sounds good," said Sandra. She added, "For a family goal, one thing I'd like to set is a goal to take a 10-day family vacation. When you were working, we rarely had time to take a meaningful family vacation without you checking your messages all the time. I want to take a vacation where the family functions as a family and we have your undivided attention."

Sandra was right. Instead of taking pure vacations, I had a tendency to tack on a family vacation to the back end of a business trip. Everybody got shortchanged. So I told Sandra, "I'm okay with that, but here's an idea on how I can get closer to the kids. How about I take a one-on-one trip with each of them? They can pick a place they want to go. How's that for undivided attention?"

"I think the kids would love that. Even though they are just about on their own now, I think they would love to spend time with you, and since they are older, it opens up more options as to what you can do with them. You could see some Broadway shows or go snowboarding in the Rockies or fishing in Canada. That's a great idea, Andrew. Write it down as a goal so you don't let it slide."

"Got it. Let's come up with another family goal. How about doing a service project as a family? We could have a family meeting and discuss as a family what's important to us. Then we could go out and volunteer our time to help others in need."

"Wow, Andrew, where is this coming from? If this is the new you, I love it," said Sandra. "I'm getting excited, and it's not just from the ideas you're coming up with."

After a detour from the goal-setting process and another loop of the George Winston CD, we got back to the Blueprinting Exercises.

"Honey, I think we should set a goal to work on these Blueprinting Exercises every week."

"If you keep acting like this, we won't need the Blueprinting Exercises," replied Sandra, with a mischievous glint in her eye.

Our playful banter reminded me of the early days of our relationship, when life and love were so much easier and fluid. It was beginning to dawn on me that time and age is no excuse for losing your sense of fun, spontaneity, and adventure.

"Goal setting at work was never this much fun," I said. "Let's come up with a few more goals, then wrap up for the day. I think we have some good family goals. Now we need some personal goals. What would you like to accomplish, honey?"

Sandra had never been a goal setter, but she seemed to know intuitively how to do it.

"It seems to me that if a goal is going to be meaningful and motivational, it has to be tied to something of value to me. Earlier, I said that my highest values were faith, family, financial security, friends, concern for others, and health, so my personal goals will all revolve around these."

"Can you come up with something specific and measurable?" I asked.

"I'd like to do a better job of staying close to your family and my family. It seems like we're all so busy that we just get together on the holidays and have an occasional phone call. They're family; we should be reaching out more."

"How are you going to measure that?" I asked her, with an emphasis on *that*.

"Andrew, not everything has to be measured," she reminded me.

Sandra seemed more into the spirit of goal setting, which is to help you focus on an objective and make progress toward it, whether it is mathematically measurable or not. I focused on traditional goal setting, which says your goals have to be very specific.

I kept my business hat on and said, "You know what I like to say, 'What gets measured gets done.'"

She wasn't pleased. "Andrew, you know what I like to say? Don't treat me like I'm an employee. I'm your wife, or have you already forgotten what just happened a few minutes ago?"

"You're right. I'm sorry."

"Apology accepted. Now what's one of your personal goals?"

It didn't take me long to come up with one. "How about I set a goal to have a new job lined up or a new business launched by 60 days from now at 12:00 P.M.?"

"I like it. It's very precise and measurable. It reminds me of what somebody once told me, 'What gets measured, gets done.'"

"Very funny, honey."

CHAPTER 15 ∎

Stan was with me the night I met Sandra, and I'll never forget that evening. We were trolling Rush Street in downtown Chicago, when I noticed a young woman out of the corner of my eye who was sitting with three friends at a popular bar. She was wearing a white blouse and tight, faded jeans—a simple but effective combination. Once she was in my sights, I watched her and became even more enamored of her outward beauty and the peaceful, easy feeling she exuded.

Mustering up my courage, I asked her to dance, and without hesitation, she said yes. As we gyrated on the dance floor to an old Elvis song, our eyes met, and I sensed that something deeper was transpiring. For the rest of the evening, Sandra and her two friends and Stan and I sat together, talking and laughing. A sensuous philosophy major from Stillwater, Minnesota, Sandra's presence that evening ignited a passion in me that I never knew I had.

Through the years, Stan and I remained good friends, although in the past couple, we hadn't seen as much of each other. He had a new girlfriend about 15 years his junior who was keeping him busy in more ways than one. Sandra and I went out with them a couple times, but as a group, we really didn't click.

Stan happened to call a few days after Sandra and I went through the Blueprinting Exercises, and he wanted to meet me for lunch. As in old times, we met at the bar where Sandra and I first met.

"Hey it's great to see you, old pal. What have you been doing to keep busy now that you're no longer at Wainwright?"

"It's been pretty boring compared to your life. I've been swinging on ropes, wading through streams, doing breathing exercises, and getting in touch with my inner self," I said.

"What? Are you going wacky on me? If anybody should be losing their marbles, it should be me. You've always been the steady one."

"No, not going wacky. Things are just a little different, that's all."

"Well, hey, here's why I wanted to meet. You and I have been friends for a long time, and we've been competing against each other in business since day one. I got to thinking: you're no longer working at Wainwright, and I have nothing tying me down at Crestone. Why don't we seriously think about starting a real estate development business together? With our experience and connections, we could build a great company and make millions. Instead of the profits going to our bosses, they'd go to our pockets. What do you think?"

There was no doubt Stan was a sharp real estate guy. He had a good nose for finding hot properties and was a great salesperson. On the deals where we'd competed head to head, our firms had each won about half of them.

"That would certainly be a major change, Stan—working with you instead of competing against you."

"That's the beauty of it. We've remained friends since college, even though we've been business competitors for most of that time. Imagine what we could accomplish being on the same team as business partners. With our track records, we could raise a substantial amount of institutional money, and I'll bet within months, we could be breaking ground on our first deal. We could even put our names on the building like Trump does. He's the king in New York. We can be the kings in Chicago, the dynamic duo, just like the old days before you got married."

I thought I had an ego, but if mine was as tall as the Old Water Tower, then his was as tall as the John Hancock building. But there was some appeal in his idea.

"Are you serious about this?"

"Absolutely. Neither of us is getting any younger. Hey, if we're going to do a big deal, now's the time. You've only got one kid left at home, and you and Sandra will be empty nesters before you know it. This new business would give you something to get excited about again."

"You're right about the timing. I'm unemployed and haven't started anything new yet. I'll tell you what, let me mull it over and talk to Sandra."

We had a filling lunch, and Stan brought me up to date on the latest real estate news. Toward the end of the conversation, I caught myself visualizing the scene from years earlier, when I first asked Sandra to dance in that same bar. The décor, along with my life, had changed dramatically since that providential meeting. I wondered . . . could this bar be the scene of two life-changing events?

Once again, I found myself apprehensive about an upcoming conversation with Sandra. The last time, it was telling her about quitting my job. This time, it was about possibly starting a new business with Stan.

CHAPTER 16

"You want to do what?" Those were the first words out of Sandra's mouth, and it went downhill from there. "What about the Blueprinting Exercises we just worked on? Didn't that mean anything to you? What about your interest in researching the residential solar energy business?"

"Sandra, think about this. Stan and I are great real estate people. We've been friends for years, and now we have a chance to work on the same team. He's great at sales, and I'm a great detail guy. We complement each other. I think it's a great fit."

"You need to do something new. Getting back into the real estate business with Stan would be no better than it was with Len. You'd be tempted to cut corners and make backroom deals with people all over again. You know I've never completely trusted Stan. He never grew up. This is a bad idea."

"Look, I need to get back to work again and make money. Stan's right—we could make millions together, and I'm surprised we never thought about getting together earlier. Do you realize what we could do with that kind of money?"

"The issue is not what we can do with that kind of money. The issue is what that kind of money does to you. You still haven't learned, have you?" Sandra's tears of hope from a few weeks ago when I quit my job now turned to tears of despair, despair that I still hadn't shed the skin of my old ways. "Go work with Stan. I don't care anymore."

I felt horrible. Sandra and I had grown closer working on the Blueprinting Exercises; then I turned right around and blew it.

CHAPTER 17

As part of my workout ritual, Tamara typically started me on the treadmill with 10 minutes of walking at 3.5 miles per hour and a 2 percent incline. At our fourth workout, after a couple moments of chitchat, she got right to the point.

"How have you been eating, Andrew?"

I was prepared. I had tried to follow my "What gets measured gets done" philosophy, and I pulled out the list of foods I'd consumed over the previous week. She carefully scanned it and was impressed with my level of detail but not with all of my choices.

"Overall, I think you've made a good start here, but there's plenty of room for improvement." She probably didn't like the chocolate candy. "People have a tendency to make dieting much harder than it really is, Andrew. Keep in mind, if you want to lose weight, you have to burn more calories than you consume."

"Does that mean I have to give up the M&M's?"

"As a personal trainer I like to put things in terms that people can relate to. An occasional bag of M&M's probably won't kill you. You may just have to exercise a little longer to maintain your ideal weight."

"I never really thought of it in those terms before."

"Most people don't. As humans, we have a tendency to live for the moment and not think of the consequences of our choices. Every choice we make has a consequence. If we choose to fill our bodies with junk food, we'll end up paying a steep price. If we choose to fill our bodies with fruits, vegetables, whole grains, nuts, fish, and the occasional lean steak, we will, as Mr. Spock says, 'Live long and prosper.'"

"Is that why so many people in our country are overweight?"

"I think it's because our society today is so competitive and fast paced. People don't have time to plan and prepare meals anymore and family dinners seem to be a thing of the past. Instead of an enriching communal experience, eating has become, for many people, an unhealthy, rushed activity. I don't mean to get on a soapbox, Andrew, but I do feel strongly about health. That's why I'm a personal trainer."

"No problem," I said. "I value your opinion—that's why I asked."

Tamara looked at my detailed food log again and gave me some additional ideas on how to eat better. She really connected with me when she explained that health is like a three-legged stool.

1. *Diet* is the first leg. What you put into your body is fuel, and the better fuel you use, the more efficiently you'll run. Imagine trying to put regular gasoline into a jet engine. It may fly but not very far and not very efficiently. Likewise, putting the wrong fuel in your body could lead to lethargy and obesity.

2. *Aerobic exercise* is the second leg. Aerobic exercise offers several benefits, including a stronger heart,

weight loss, and the release of endorphins. Endorphins are "happy" chemicals released by the brain. They help you feel euphoric and reduce stress and anxiety. Being aerobically fit also boosts your immune system, so you'll be less susceptible to minor colds and the flu.

3. *Strength training* is the third leg. After about age 35, we lose roughly half a pound of muscle a year. Diet and aerobic exercise is important, but if that's all you do, you'll end up thin and weak. Strength training will keep your muscles active and growing and help keep your fat down.

For 45 minutes, Tamara led me through a full-body workout on the weight machines as she interspersed her words of wisdom.

"This feels pretty light," I said, as I did 12 reps on the bench press machine.

"That's by design. One of the biggest mistakes people make when they start an exercise program is they overdo it. I promise you, you'll be sore tomorrow, even though we're going pretty light today."

"But I feel like a sissy. See that woman over there; she's lifting more than I am. Can we increase the weight? This is embarrassing." Still ruled by my ego, I was comparing myself to other people.

Tamara said we'd start with a light full-body workout for the first few weeks, so I could get my muscles into the groove of stress. "Muscles grow because you put them under stress. During the workout, you actually break down the muscle, and then after the workout, when you are resting, the muscle repairs itself, and that's how they grow," she said.

"You think my muscles are going to grow after this measly workout?" I asked. I'm sure I wasn't the first client she'd ever had that was a little difficult. To her credit, she knew exactly how to deal with me.

"How long did it take you to become an expert in the real estate business?" she asked.

"Probably eight to ten years, why?"

"Just like when you got into the real estate business, you have to start somewhere and then build on it. These exercises may feel easy, but they're sending a signal to your body that something is changing. That change will build over time, and as we develop this muscular base for you, we can gradually raise the weight level."

She was probably right, but I was impatient. "You're the boss," I said with some resignation.

As we wrapped up the session, I noticed I was wiping sweat from my face. "It feels good to sweat again," I told her.

"So maybe it wasn't such an easy day after all?" she replied.

"Well," I stammered, "it's not that big of a sweat," and we both chuckled.

After a quick stop in the locker room, we rendezvoused at the front counter.

"Being in the real estate business, I know you can appreciate leverage, Andrew. To leverage the workout you just did, let's pick out a protein shake so we can give your body some nutrients to repair the muscles you just broke down. This one's on me."

Not wanting to pass up a freebie, I surveyed the menu and was surprised to find how many different ways you could make protein powder look tasty.

"How about the strawberry protein with blueberries, raspberries, and a banana?"

"An excellent choice. Maybe you know this, but blueberries are one of the best foods you can eat. They have lots of cancer-fighting antioxidants, and they're so tasty, I put a scoopful in my fruit smoothie each morning," said Tamara.

"I'll drink to that."

CHAPTER 18

After sleeping in the spare bedroom for a couple of nights, I decided that it was more important to try to patch things up with Sandra than to try to make millions with Stan. I asked her to forgive me, yet again, for my bad judgment.

"In baseball, you only get three strikes, and then you're out. You're perilously close to that third strike, Andrew." Even for Sandra there was a limit to her patience.

I called Stan and told him that I had decided not to go into business with him. He said I was passing up a great opportunity and that I'd regret it someday. "Money can make up for a lot of other problems," he told me.

He sounded a lot like Len. Both Stan and Len seemed to think money was all that mattered to me, and based on my behavior over the past 20 years, I suppose that was a logical conclusion.

With the real estate bug now out of my system, I finally got serious about researching climate change and the need for solar energy. As I researched it, I became fascinated by the theories and purported facts about this potentially catastrophic situation. Relegated to the lunatic fringe not all that long ago, more and more respected scientists were coming to the conclusion that humanity is changing the environment—and not in a good way.

I remembered reading a quote that said all ideas pass through three stages. First, they're ridiculed. Second, they're violently opposed. Then third, they're accepted as being self-evident. Climate change seemed to be fitting that pattern.

The more research I did, the more excited I became about starting a solar energy business to help relieve the climate change problem. I read numerous books, consulted with local experts in Chicago, and even went to a couple of climate change symposiums. I began to feel as though something was pulling me in this direction. As I weighed the pros and cons, they seemed to tilt in favor of moving forward.

However, on the negative side, the thought of starting my own business was scary. What if I failed? I wasn't very good at dealing with setbacks. Heck, I was still having trouble dealing with quitting my job at Wainwright.

As I thought through this business decision, Sandra and I moved forward with our financial planning goals. We had a second meeting with Hank to go over the wealth plan. We spent the first few minutes updating him on the results of our Blueprinting Exercise. I tucked my tail between my legs and told him he was right about how helpful the exercises could be. He just smiled and said he was very happy it worked out. He also said that Blueprinting is not just a one-time deal.

"As things change in your life, revisit the exercises and make adjustments as appropriate."

During the rest of the meeting, Hank and his team went over the wealth plan. I was very impressed, because it seemed as though Hank had really listened to us. His plan addressed all our needs, including the following:

- *Cash flow.* He showed us how much money we were spending and how long our existing assets would last at a 4 percent withdrawal rate.

- *Investments.* He compared our existing investments to his proposed portfolio and showed how through intelligent diversification, we could improve our odds of getting a better return without taking any additional risk.

- *Taxes.* He recommended some new investments that would help us reduce our tax burden and provide us with tax-free income.

- *Risk management.* He identified some holes in our insurance protection that he could solve rather easily.

- *Estate planning.* He had some ideas on how to minimize our potential estate taxes and how we could make charitable contributions in the most tax-advantaged way.

Along the way, Sandra and I asked a few questions, and Hank and his team had good answers. The plan made sense, so we gave Hank the okay to proceed. It turned out to be a surprisingly painless process. His staff did a great job of handling all the paperwork and transferring our assets to the new accounts. He even arranged meetings with an accountant and an estate-planning attorney to go over our tax and estate situation. Sandra and I couldn't have been more pleased with the service.

On the drive home from the office, Sandra commented on how much better she felt now that we had a financial plan in place that covered all aspects of our situation.

I said to her, "You're just happy because, with this insurance policy, I'm worth more to you dead than alive."

Without missing a beat she said, "At least I can laugh all the way to the bank."

She found that a little more humorous than I did.

CHAPTER 19

    I continued to work through my business idea. Sandra was a great sounding board as she listened intently, asked good questions, and challenged my commitment. When it was all over, she gave me the thumbs-up. She said she completely supported the idea and felt that it was something I needed to do. That really was the tipping point. With her encouragement, I finished the due diligence, put together a business plan, and checked the family finances. All systems were go.

    To lessen the risk of starting a business in an area where I didn't have a lot of experience, I decided to buy a franchise called Environmental Partner Solar Energy. Essentially, we install commercial and residential solar energy systems. Getting up and running set me back about $120,000, including the franchise fee, opening the store, and working capital. To help launch the business, I talked to Hank, and he helped me with a couple things. First, he helped me wade through all the different governmental organizations that offered small business loans, tax advice, and start-up help to businesses like mine. Second, he helped me set up our bookkeeping system so we could accurately track our financials. With him in my corner, I felt that we were giving this business every chance to succeed.

    The grand opening happened in November, exactly four months after I quit my job at Wainwright. However, it was not exactly a standing-room-only event. We sent direct mail pieces to the neighboring zip codes and that brought in a few people, mostly tire kickers, or in this case, "panel kickers." Fortunately, one of the regional trainers from the franchiser was in town and could answer some of the more technical questions.

I was pleasantly surprised to see Edwin and Ava Luther at our grand opening. As a courtesy, I'd sent them an invitation, even though I didn't expect them to make the drive from Wisconsin. Upon seeing them, I gave them both a hug. It wasn't my normal greeting, but something just overcame me at that moment.

"It's so great to see you two, and thank you so much for making the trip. You know you didn't have to come here."

"We know, but you've been so good to us. Best way to thank someone is to show up in person, that's what I say. And Ava, she hasn't traveled much, but she's feeling better."

I looked at Ava and gave her a big smile. She smiled back and said, "Mr. Craver, there's another reason why we're here. We want ya to come up and put some of these panel things on our house. We want to be one of your first customers."

It just about brought tears to my eyes. Seeing how well Ava had progressed warmed my heart. The fact that the easement and the land trust deal was completed was also a great feeling for all of us.

Business was slow those first few months. We inundated the airwaves with an expensive radio campaign that kept some new business coming in the door. Newspaper advertising also helped. However, just as when I started in the real estate business, I felt myself getting sucked right back into the trap of working long hours and putting my family on the back burner. As a neophyte in the solar energy business, I had to immerse myself in the details. The combination of learning the business plus trying to build the business meant long hours away from Sandra and Kevin. The business wasn't profitable, so I had to write a check each month to keep it afloat. That was stressful.

Even though the business was tough, something felt very right about it. I felt that I really was making a difference. I was doing something positive for the world, and I was helping other people express their need to do something positive for the world. With my clients, we were becoming catalysts for change, and it was inspiring.

CHAPTER 20

Although I was afraid I couldn't afford it, following my business plan, I hired a hippy-looking, ponytailed, 42-year-old named Colin who seemed to know his stuff when it came to solar panels. Hank had given me some informal business advice, saying that one of the best ways to grow your business was to hire staff before you can afford to. The theory was, by hiring staff, you'd free yourself to spend time on the things that you do best and that adds the most value to your company. He conveniently left out one other part of the theory. Hiring staff before you can afford it puts tremendous pressure on you to perform. When you have to meet payroll, you are motivated to work hard and generate business.

Colin turned out to be a surprisingly good hire. He was a hard worker and dependable, and he wasn't afraid to get up on the roofs and install the panels. Yet to look at him, you would have never guessed that he'd be an A+ employee. I realized that I had stereotyped him and nearly missed an opportunity to grow my business. It reminded me of the 1970 song "Signs" about the long-haired guy who got the job after disguising his freaky appearance.

As I spent more time getting the business off the ground, my regular trips to the gym started to slip. Although I understood the importance of working out, it was still expendable—at least I thought it was. Tamara had been through this before. A new client comes in, they get all excited about working out, but then reality sets in, and they fade away. However, Tamara had a plan for me.

"Hello, stranger," she said, on my first visit after a two-week absence.

"I know it's probably a cliché. Hard-driving man gets excited about working out, takes it seriously for a few months, and then gradually loses interest and moves on to something else. You've seen this before haven't you, Tamara?" With a sly smile, she nodded in agreement.

"Andrew, do you like challenges?"

"Do fish swim?"

"I thought so. Here's your homework for today. I want you to set a challenging physical goal. The key is, the goal has to be motivating. It has to be so exciting that you will be compelled to keep your appointments with me because you know you have to be in great shape to accomplish it."

"I get it. I'll think about that."

"Don't think too long. I'd like you to let me know the goal by the end of today's workout."

"You know, Tamara, you're good. You can be a bit pushy, but you know when to push my buttons and when to step back and provide encouragement. You're politely aggressive. I like that."

"Thank you. I had good teachers."

At the end of the workout, Tamara led me through a breathing exercise. "Slow down. Relax. Find your soul." Interestingly, rather than feeling self-conscious, I felt more in tune with what my body was telling me . . . and it was telling me I needed to relax.

"Andrew, in addition to coming up with a motivational goal, I want you to commit to me that you will perform this breathing exercise once a day."

"I'll try."

"No 'try'—do."

"There you go again, Tamara, you sound like Yoda." We both laughed.

"Okay, Andrew, have you come up with a motivational goal?" Tamara wasn't about to let me off the hook.

"I have."

"Drum roll please."

"I want to climb Mount Rainier."

"Mount Rainier, that certainly is a challenging goal. Why is that motivating to you?"

"It's funny. When I was in high school, I took a trip to Seattle and arrived late at night. That morning, when I stepped outside, the sun was shining, and I saw this huge, snow-capped mountain taking up the bulk of the southern sky. I was awestruck and said to myself that someday I would come back and climb it. Well, life got in the way, and some-day never arrived."

"So you think maybe now is that 'someday'?"

"No 'think'—know."

"Now you're sounding like Yoda," said Tamara with a nod of approval.

"Yeah, I'd actually forgotten about it until now, but your challenge brought it back to my consciousness. That trip to Seattle years ago was during a very unhappy time in my life. In some ways, my life is so different today, but in other ways, I feel like I've just relived my dad's life.

Like him, I grew my career while I grew away ⟨from my⟩
wife and kids."

"How do you think climbing the mountain w⟨ill change⟩
you?"

"I don't know about 'change me,' but it will give me
something fun to talk about at parties."

"And after your 15 minutes of fame, then what?"

"I haven't thought that far."

"Do you think all the hard training you'll have to do to
make it to the top and back will be worth it just so you have
something unique and impressive to talk about at cocktail
parties?"

"Well, when you phrase it that way, probably not."

"That kind of reason wouldn't get you much past the
trailhead. Andrew, I think climbing Mount Rainier could be
the kind of goal that transforms you, but you need to get
your ego out of it and get your soul into it."

"What do you mean by that?"

"Whenever you set a goal, it can't be about inflating your
sense of self-importance. Goals need to be matched with your
values and have a purpose beyond the obvious."

"That's funny. Sandra said basically the same thing. Is
this a female conspiracy?"

"If we're conspiring, it's to help you grow, Andrew. Since
we're being open here, I want you to know one of my goals.
I'm a personal trainer, and I help people get in better physical shape, but my real purpose is to help people gain a deeper
understanding of their soul. I use health as a way to help
people get to the root of their essence."

"Okay." I didn't quite know how to respond to that.

"I encourage you to do more research about mountain
climbing. Read some of the more philosophical books about

climbing mountains and see if any of those writers and climbers connect with you."

"Will do."

As I started to walk toward the locker room, she said, "One more thing, find a partner who can train and climb with you. That extra accountability will help you through the tough times."

CHAPTER 21 ∎

"You want to climb Mount Rainier? If this is a continuation of your midlife crisis, wouldn't it be safer to buy a little red Corvette?" Sandra asked.

Sandra was skeptical and for good reason. I had never shown any interest in climbing mountains in the past, so I was hitting her cold with it. She also reminded me that we still hadn't taken the 10-day family vacation that we'd discussed during the Blueprinting Exercises. I told her maybe we could do both.

After spending some time on the Internet and at the library browsing through some climbing books, I discovered that climbing Rainier as a novice was doable but would require tremendous preparation. I also discovered that for some people, it's a one-way trip. Statistics from the National Park Service said that, on average, about two to three people a year die trying to climb the mountain. I'd also read that back in 1981, a massive avalanche entombed 11 people in a permanent grave. Clearly, this was not going to be a cakewalk, and I had to be prepared—physically and mentally.

As far as the more philosophical thoughts on climbing, what stuck me was how climbing breaks life down to its most fundamental level. Here I am in a 9,000-square-foot house with lots of stuff, yet when you climb, everything you need to live fits neatly in a 50-pound backpack. When you break life down to its essentials, it doesn't weigh much.

Sandra reluctantly gave in. "I can't stop you, and you're going to do what you want anyway."

With that behind me, I set my sights on finding a climbing partner, and I knew just the right person—Dr. Graham. He agreed to meet up with me for a hike, and as we walked through the forest near his office, I just flat out asked him.

"Dr. Graham, I know you stay in good physical condition, and I was wondering if you are up for a big challenge."

"What did you have in mind?"

"I'm planning on climbing Mount Rainier next June, and it would be more fun with a partner. Would you like to train with me and do the climb?"

There was a noticeable silence before he responded. "Mount Rainier."

"Yeah, you're familiar with it aren't you?"

"Yes, Andrew, I am familiar with Mount Rainier. Are you sure you know what you're getting yourself into climbing that mountain?"

"I think so. Several companies guide neophytes like me up to the top. They say anybody in good shape with strong determination and a little luck can make it."

"Rainier should not be underestimated. It's created many widows over the years and left a trail of tears in its wake."

"I know, a little danger adds to the allure."

"You can find danger in places other than mountains. Why Rainier?"

"Tamara asked me that same question. At first I told her it would be for bragging rights, but after I thought about it, I realized it's a big challenge, it will force me out of my comfort zone, and who knows, maybe I'll have a religious experience or something during the climb."

There was another long pause as we continued walking. Dr. Graham then picked up four large sticks and gave two to me. "Here, we'll need to practice walking with poles if we ever have any hope of making it to the top."

It was his way of saying yes.

CHAPTER 22

For all my imperfections, when I get going on something, I put everything I have into it. Training for the climb was no exception. When I wasn't working—which, by the way, wasn't often—I was training.

Over the next few months, Dr. Graham and I followed a strict training regime of running, backpacking, weight lifting, and even yoga—thanks to Tamara. I was impressed with Dr. Graham's physical condition. For a man in his mid-50s, he had the strength and agility of a man 20 years younger.

With no mountains here in Chicago, we tried to simulate mountain climbing as best we could by filling our packs with a 40-pound bag of salt and then walking on a treadmill set at a 15-degree incline. By the end of those workouts, I felt as though we had sweated out about 40 pounds of salt.

Reaching the summit of Rainier became an overriding goal for me. I got on the Internet and downloaded a picture of it, then pasted it into a PowerPoint® slide. I superimposed my written goals on the slide, then printed it in color and laminated it. I placed a copy in my shower and kept one in my car and in my carrying case. I did the same thing with my compelling vision and my personal mission statement, and each morning before I shaved, I picked them up and read them. I found that was a great way to start the day.

With Tamara's help, I set specific training goals in terms of the number of hours per week, the intensity, and my heart rate level. Weight lifting was important, too, and we placed an extra emphasis on core strength, the shoulders, and the back.

Training with Dr. Graham was an intellectual exercise. He wasn't a loud, joking kind of guy; instead, he was cerebral and task oriented. The more time I spent with him, the more I realized what a complex person he was. Never one to talk much, he had an uncanny way of getting the most out of the few words he spoke.

When it came to Mount Rainier, Dr. Graham really knew his stuff. Almost as well as someone who had been there before. I had definitely picked a great climbing partner.

In working with Tamara, I became a believer in the benefits of reciting daily affirmations. From reading books and just observing life, I came up with a few affirmations that I wrote down and posted above my desk. One day, the subject of affirmations came up when I was training with Dr. Graham, and he asked me what mine were.

"I've got four, I said.

1. I put my family first, and they bring great joy into my life.
2. The price of progress is the pain of change, and I am willing to endure the pain.
3. Each day, I find happiness in doing something nice for someone who can never repay me.
4. I learn as though I'll live forever, and I live as though I'll die tomorrow.

"Well said, Andrew. You recognize the importance of Sandra, Kellie, and Kevin, but understand that family extends beyond blood relatives. I'm not married and only have one brother, but everyone I come in contact with is part of my family. We're all related," he said.

I had trouble just taking care of my immediate family, let alone trying to include everyone I knew in my family circle, but his point was valid.

CHAPTER 23

■

While my training went well, my business and my relationship with Sandra and the kids stayed stuck in neutral. Between trying to build the business and training for the climb, I had very little time, or I should say I devoted very little time, to deepening my relationship with them. Once again, it was all about me.

Frustrated, Sandra cornered me one day. "Andrew," she began. I know when she calls me by my first name instead of "sweetie" or "honey" that I'm in for it. "Our life revolves around you. You're either working or training, and when you're not doing those things, you want to relax and have some time for yourself. Whatever happened to that vision and mission we developed? Didn't that mean anything to you?"

To some men, this might have come off as nagging, but from Sandra, I knew she had the best intentions. And frankly, she was right. My kids had essentially grown up without me, and Sandra was trying to help me see that the most important things in my life were not really things. Sandra and the kids had loved me unconditionally for years. Unfortunately, the way I paid them back, or at least justified my lack of engagement with them, was to say I was off working so I could make a good income to provide them with things. I still wasn't getting it that the "thing" she and the kids wanted was not a "thing," rather it was me—my time, attention, and love.

To try to remedy the situation, I said, "Why don't we plan on taking a mental health day on Friday. The four of us can go up to Door County for a three-day weekend, since Kellie doesn't have Friday classes. We'll just try to relax and reconnect."

"That would be wonderful," said Sandra. "Those are the kinds of things I wish you'd come up with without prompting from me. As I told you before, just seeing you with the kids and interacting with them, I find that attractive."

There's no doubt I was a slow learner. Sandra had been telling me for years what she found attractive, and I'd never picked up on it. Had I been more perceptive, our life might have turned out much differently. Unfortunately, I kept working hard and kept up the training. Shedding my selfishness was an agonizingly slow process.

CHAPTER 24   ■

Several uneventful months passed as I continued to work on the business, train, and try to focus on being a better husband and father. As the final week prior to the big climb arrived, I went over all the details again. My copy of *Mount Rainier: A Climbing Guide* was dog-eared and full of yellow highlighting. Earlier, our guiding company had sent us a detailed checklist of all the stuff we'd need. Fortunately, they had a rental shop where we could rent most of our gear, but I had purchased a few items that I thought I could use even when I was off the mountain.

The night before we left, I laid out all my gear and triple-checked my checklist to make sure I didn't forget anything. Amazingly, it all fit neatly into my big suitcase and my 5,000-cubic-inch backpack. That evening, I went to bed and visualized myself successfully standing on the summit with my arms raised over my head, ice axe in hand, and the sun brightly shining down on me.

Before I fell asleep, Sandra gave me a little laminated piece of paper about the size of a business card. On one side was a picture of her and the kids and on the other side were a few of her words of wisdom.

See but not with your eyes.
Listen but not with your ears.

Feel but not with your hands.
Climb but not with your legs.
Know but not with your mind.

Touched by her thoughtfulness, I told her I'd put it in my jacket pocket and take it with me to the top. We kissed goodnight, rolled over, and tried to sleep.

In the morning, after loading up the SUV, I let Sandra know where our will and insurance policies were located, just in case I came back in a casket. I kidded her that if I didn't come back alive, she'd have plenty of insurance money to help offset her grief. She kidded me back and said that would be a good trade-off.

I was surprised that she wasn't a little more concerned for my safety, because people do die climbing Mount Rainier. Kevin, ironically, was more concerned than Sandra. He actually gave me a hug and said to be careful. The hug gave me mixed emotions. On one hand, I was happy that my son showed that emotion toward me. On the other hand, I was embarrassed that he initiated it instead of me. Turns out, Sandra wasn't the only family member who could teach me something.

With perfect timing, Kellie called me on my cell phone from school. "Be careful, Dad, I love you," were her last words.

"I love you, too, honey." I love you, too.

CHAPTER 25

I picked up Dr. Graham at his neatly kept, middle-class house and helped him put his gear and luggage in the back of my SUV. Dr. Graham opened the front passenger-side door and put one leg in the car while pausing for a moment and looking at his house. I couldn't see his eyes, but it struck me as odd that he just stood there for a moment before he got in and sat down. He probably wanted to make sure he hadn't forgotten anything.

Traditionally, the weather on Mount Rainier starts to change in mid-June and becomes relatively pleasant for the summer. I'd been checking the weather reports regularly, and the prognosis looked good. The day before our June 20 flight out of Chicago, the mountain received a foot and a half of new powder, but then a high-pressure system was supposed to roll in and keep the skies clear for a few days.

As we neared Seattle, my six-month obsession came into luminous view. Even from 30,000 feet, the mountain—smothered in a coat of white—dominated the landscape. I turned to Dr. Graham and gave him a look that said, "This is going to take a major effort to reach the top."

My apprehension rose geometrically as we made the 90-minute drive from Sea-Tac to Ashford, our home for the first two nights. With every passing minute, the mountain began to grow, until it practically filled the view from the windshield of our rental car. Then, about 60 minutes into the drive, the summit just disappeared, cloaked in a menacing-looking cloud. It looked as if someone had just sliced it cleanly at about the 10,000-foot level. A few blinks later, the cloud dispersed, and it was back to normal. Dr. Graham looked at me and said, "Andrew, that cloud is a good reminder that we may have done all we can to prepare, but in the end, we're not in control of what happens up there." I nodded in agreement and wondered silently if he could sense that my usual confidence was sliding away.

Later that afternoon, we arrived at the Bunkhouse in Ashford and promptly went to the rental shop to pick up the rest of our gear. After grabbing a bite to eat, we went back to our rooms, organized our gear, and tried to get a good night's rest.

CHAPTER 26

Having never climbed before, we had to participate in a climbing school on our first day on the mountain. After making the 45-minute drive to the trailhead at the Paradise Inn parking lot, we got out of the van and sorted our gear. A short time later, we laced up boots and strapped on our backpacks. Even though it was early June, we stepped off the parking lot and into deep snow. Thirty minutes later, we found ourselves at the top of a hill and in the hands of our expert guides Peter and Ty. They taught us some of the basics of mountain climbing

One of the day's key objectives was to learn how to self-arrest, which would be very useful in case we fell. Essentially, we practiced falling down a slope, then rolling onto our stomachs while trying to use our body weight to bury the pick of the axe into the snow and ice. When used successfully, the axe acted as a brake and "arrested" our slide. To add some adrenaline, as soon as we fell, we had to yell, "Falling!" several times. We practiced falling both individually and as a roped team. Peter said, "If you learn nothing else from today, make sure you learn how to arrest a fall. I don't want any of you sliding into oblivion." No problem, I thought. I've got this part nailed.

The weather was perfect, very sunny and warm, but the snow was slushy. It felt great to be on the mountain and get a feel for what to expect. At the end of the day, I was pumped. I'd picked up the skills easily, and I began to think that this climb wasn't going to be very hard after all.

To my surprise, Dr. Graham seemed like a natural mountain climber. He quickly picked up everything the guides taught us, and he was effective at self-arresting. With those skills, he would make a good rope partner. Things couldn't be more perfect.

That evening, we ate at the café and mingled with some of the other climbers. It was quite a contrast. One climber had just returned from the summit and was all excited about telling us, while his partner was dehydrated and very exhausted. The exhausted climber didn't have the energy to eat and spent most of the time hunched over the table with his head in his hands. At another table, I struck up a conversation with a guide and his girlfriend. She told me she had climbed the mountain four times in the past year. My body language gave away what I was thinking. If there was any doubt about my ability to get to the top, it ended right there. If this petite young woman could climb it four times, then there was nothing for me to fear.

Ever the wise one, Dr. Graham turned to me and in a rather somber tone said, "Mountains have a way of turning hubris into humility."

Back in our spartan room, I didn't have to count sheep to fall asleep. Between the climbing school and the fresh mountain air, I was ready to hit the pillow and get a few hours sleep before the main event began.

By 10:00 the next morning, Dr. Graham and I had eaten, gotten organized, and joined our party of six, plus two guides, on the Paradise Inn trailhead. Starting at an elevation of 5,420 feet, we methodically put one foot in front of the other as we slowly made the five-hour, 4.5-mile hike to the 10,000-foot way station called Camp Muir. At our first rest stop about an hour into the hike, I turned to Peter and asked him why he was going so slowly. "Not everybody is in as good of shape as you are, Andrew," he said. Yep, even he could tell this was a breeze for me. I made a mental note to thank Tamara for pushing me over the past 10 months.

Dr. Graham seemed to be holding up okay. We briefly chatted during the three stops on our way to Camp Muir, but for the most part, we just rehydrated, snapped some pictures, and absorbed the view. It couldn't have been more beautiful. Despite traveling on snow the whole time, I wore shorts and a high-tech shirt that wicked away my sweat. Good thing I had a hat, glacier glasses, sunscreen, and lip balm.

At 3:00 P.M. sharp, we reached Camp Muir. Barely winded, I turned to Dr. Graham and said, "Let's keep going. This is a piece of cake." His look told me that he was not amused.

CHAPTER 27

With three hours before lights out, I pulled out my cell phone and called Sandra. "You should see what I see, honey. It's like a different world up here, and I can see Mount St. Helens and Mount Adams in the distance."

"Take some pictures, and we can turn it into a family event watching the slide show," she said.

"The climb's been easy so far. My legs were strong. I didn't get winded and had no altitude sickness. Maybe I should have been a mountain-climbing guide instead of a real estate expert. This is cool."

Sandra tried to keep me from getting overconfident. "Remember, the hardest part is yet to come, so don't congratulate yourself just yet." Before I could respond, the line went dead, and I couldn't get another signal. We didn't even get to say good-bye.

A few minutes later, the guides called us back together for some last-minute instructions and preparations. By 6:00 P.M., we retreated to our hut and tried to get a few hours of rest. I grabbed a top bunk and, lying on my back, stared at the ceiling. I tried to imagine what the next 24 hours would look like. Would it be as easy as the last 24? Would I struggle but still reach the summit? Would I get altitude sickness? Would the weather hold?

At 11:30 P.M., Peter woke us up, and for the next hour and a half, we got dressed; ate; put on our avalanche beacons, boots, crampons, helmets, and headlamps; and tied ourselves into the rope. Peter was first on the rope, followed by me, then Dr. Graham. Ty led the second rope team. Before leaving the relative comfort of the hut, Dr. Graham and I shook hands while looking at each other's faces, eerily illuminated by the bright headlamps.

About 10 minutes into the climb, as we were crossing the Cowlitz Glacier, we heard a loud, rumbling noise that sounded like thunder. We all looked up the mountain, with our headlamps scanning the glacier and the nearby Cathedral Rocks, to see if this was the end of life as we knew it. "Falling! Falling!" I heard from somewhere up in front of me. Immediately, I fell to the ice and with the weight of my body dug the pick of my axe in as far as it would go. I buried my face to protect it from whatever was about to come. My adrenaline surged, and my body stiffened as I waited for the mountain to make its next move.

CHAPTER 28

After what seemed like an eternity, the jerk on my rope from a helplessly sliding climber or the blast from an oncoming avalanche never arrived. As suddenly as we heard the sound, it stopped. We got up, took a roll call, and kept climbing. I decided that the alarm was the mountain's way of letting me know who was in charge. A few moments later, we came across a slew of rocks and chunks of ice. Had we started our climb a few minutes earlier, we would have had a very different outcome.

Once past the Cowlitz Glacier, we made it to Cathedral Rocks, which is a huge rock formation that runs vertically up the mountain. We had to bisect it at a place called Cathedral Gap, which required us to go up and over the rocks. It was steep and a hassle to climb in crampons.

We effectively negotiated Cathedral Gap and then climbed a little farther up on good snow before stopping at the 11,100-foot Ingraham Flats for our first break. We were about one hour into the climb. I felt fine, but Dr. Graham seemed a bit nervous. At each break, we put on our parka, ate, drank water, and then packed up again. The 10 minutes went very fast. Peter warned us that the next leg was much more difficult and longer and that if we didn't feel good now, we should let him know. He also told us that the next section of the climb was the place where the 11 climbers had died back in 1981. That wasn't exactly comforting.

Clearly focused on the task at hand, we made it across the Ingraham Glacier and up the spine of the steep, dangerous rocky outcrop known as Disappointment Cleaver. At times, we walked along a narrow ledge with a wall on our left side and a cliff on our right. Because it was dark, I had no idea how far I'd fall if I slipped or took a bad step. By climbing in the dark, you can't see the danger and you can't see the crevasses, so you don't know how scared you should be.

Our second rest stop occurred at the top of the cleaver. Everybody was quiet and trying to complete their business efficiently. By now, I was starting to get tired. It was 3:30 in the morning, and I was more than 12,000 feet up on a barren, frozen, windy volcano. How could I have thought this would be fun?

All too soon, it was time to pack up and keep climbing. We climbed a zigzag path for the next hour as we negotiated crevasses and the steep terrain. At just over 13,000 feet, we took our third and final break. At this point, the altitude started to take effect, and I lost my appetite. It was frustrating at how long it took to do simple tasks. I was so busy taking care of myself that I didn't even talk to Dr. Graham.

The final push to the summit was steep and scary, as Peter led us around gaping cracks in the ice. It was only 15 degrees, and with the wind slamming us at about 25 miles per hour, I was having trouble staying warm. My fingers and toes were tingling. By the time we reached the low side of the summit crater, I was tired and punch-drunk from the altitude. Unfortunately, the true summit—Columbia Crest, was another 25-minute hike across the summit crater and a 250-foot elevation gain.

My moment of truth had arrived. I could rest for an hour at the low end of the summit crater or suck it up and keep going to the true summit. While I debated, I put my hands in my coat pocket to keep them warm. I felt something in one of the pockets, so I pulled it out. It was Sandra's laminated card. As I looked at my smiling family and read Sandra's inspiring words on the other side, it gave me an extra surge of energy. "I'm going," I said as I looked at Dr. Graham. After a deep breath, he got up, too.

With no crevasses in the summit crater, we put our packs down and unroped. Exhausted but determined, Dr. Graham and I made the trek, and 25 minutes later, we were standing at 14,410 feet, on top of the most heavily glaciated mountain in the lower 48 states. We took the obligatory victory picture and held our axes in the air. I had thought about this moment for the past six months, and now it was here. Strangely though, rather than high-fiving everybody in sight, my thought was: how in the world am I going to make it down from here? Physically depleted, I was in no mood to celebrate.

Before stepping off the summit, Dr. Graham looked at me and between pants said, "Andrew, look around you. From the top of the mountain, you have a new perspective. Remember what the writer René Daumal, author of *Mount Analogue,* said about climbing:

> *One climbs, one sees.*
> *One descends, one sees no longer, but one has seen.*
> *There is an art of conducting oneself in the lower regions by the memory of what one saw higher up.*
> *When one can no longer see, one can at least still know.*

He paused, looked straight at me, and said, "You know, Andrew. You know."

"Know what?" I asked. "Know what?" It was too late; Dr. Graham had already started walking across the crater to begin the descent.

CHAPTER 29

While walking across the crater to regain the trail back to Camp Muir, some clouds blew through and made the landscape surreal. One minute it was sunny; the next, I couldn't see 10 feet in front of me as the clouds completely obscured my view. I briefly lost sight of Dr. Graham. Rainier is so big, it creates its own weather. The mountain is actually a dormant volcano, and there are vents all around the rim that continuously emit steam. Peter told us earlier that if a storm strands you on the summit, you can curl up next to one of those vents and stay warm.

By the time we left the summit, it was shortly after 8:00 A.M.

Peter said that the descent would take about half as long as the ascent, and he wasn't kidding. The pace he set was fast, and with the snow starting to melt, I plunged into it with each step. I lost my balance a few times and fell in place as my legs slid out from under me. By the time I got to the first break at the top of Disappointment Cleaver, my legs were like noodles, and I was seriously wondering how I was going to make it all the way back to the trailhead at Paradise that day.

My appetite slowly started to come back, and I was able to choke down some energy mix and a few swigs of water at that first break. Dr. Graham and I were so busy and tired during our short break that we only locked eyes once, and we had no energy to talk.

Going down Disappointment Cleaver in the daylight was heart pounding. With steep slopes and huge crevasses beckoning if we fell, we were only one slip away from our next life. The only good thing about the Cleaver was at certain spots, it was so treacherous, we had to pause for a moment while a slower rope team made their way down. The brief rests were just enough to refresh me.

At the bottom of the Cleaver, we had to make a quick dash across the Ingraham Glacier before our next rest stop at Ingraham Flats. Our rope team, which had been short-roped going down the Cleaver, began to stretch out across the Ingraham Glacier. Peter led, followed by me about 60 feet behind, and Dr. Graham, another 60 feet behind me, brought up the rear.

Suddenly I was overcome by a deafening sound.

What the hell is that? Avalanche, run, run, run!

Before I could process what was happening, chunks of ice began to pelt me as if I were a pinball in a game gone berserk.

FALLING, FALLING, FALLING.

I tried to self-arrest but to no avail.

Where am I?

Sliding uncontrollably down the roaring mountain, I was tumbling and flailing amidst the snow and blocks of ice. Suddenly, I came to a violent stop when my rope became taut. There was dead silence and darkness. I was partially buried face down in snow and ice, bloodied but alive. I tried to move but the weight of the ice trapped me. Then the panic of being buried alive set in, triggering a dormant Herculean strength. I broke free of my temporary grave, thankful that I was spared yet hyperventilating from my close brush with death.

Dazed, I stood up and noticed that the sun was still shining but the immediate landscape of the mountain had changed dramatically. A mangled web of ice chunks had replaced the smooth snow.

I saw Peter running toward me. He yelled, "Are you okay?" I told him I was but I was scared to death. He then started pointing at me like a madman. It took me a few seconds before realizing that he wanted me to look behind me. As I turned around, I was horrified to discover that a 15-foot longer slide would have put me over the edge of a gaping chasm in the glacier. Ominously, the rope connected to my backside led directly over the edge. Frantically and instinctively, I lunged toward the edge and pulled on the rope, but there was no resistance. There, 20 feet below the lip of the crevasse, the rope dangled among a jumbled mass of snow and ice. A block of ice had cut it cleanly.

Dr. Graham? Dr. Graham!

A well-trained guide, Peter quickly reached me to double-check that I was okay.

Where's Dr. Graham?

He radioed for help, then pounded an anchor into the snow. Before I came fully to my senses, Peter had already rappelled into the crevasse.

Where's Dr. Graham?

While he searched, I was yelling for Dr. Graham. The only reply was my echo. Within minutes, several other climbers and rescue personnel had arrived on the scene, and it became a beehive of activity. After searching thoroughly, Peter climbed out of the crevasse and gave me the news I already knew in my heart. "It doesn't look good. I'm sorry. There's really nothing more you can do up here, so why don't you head back down. The park ranger will want to talk to you for the accident report."

Dr. Graham was gone, permanently entombed under tons and tons of glacial ice. I fell to my knees, sobbing and wailing.

No, no, no. This can't be happening. Dr. Graham, Dr. Graham.

CHAPTER 30

I was in shock as the helicopter came to transport me down to the parking lot of the Paradise Inn where head climbing ranger "Gator" Gonzalez was waiting to interview me. Sitting in the helicopter during the brief flight felt like an out-of-body experience. I was up high surveying a scene below me where my friend lay buried. Never again would I hear his soothing voice. Never again would I walk with him through the forest for an aerial meeting. Never again would I benefit from his wise counsel.

Never again.

There wasn't much to tell Gator. One second I was absorbed in the moment, exhausted and trying to traverse the glacier. Then, in an instant, fury, ice, sliding, then silence, then death. Life changed in an instant. Dr. Graham's . . . and mine.

"His name was Martin Graham. Is that correct?" asked Gator.

"Yes, Dr. Martin Graham."

"How old was he?"

"About 56."

Gator looked up and paused for a moment, as if he was thinking. Then he looked at me and said, "That fits. It was him."

"What the hell are you talking about? What fits?"

"He didn't tell you?"

"Tell me what?" He put his clipboard down and took a deep breath.

"Andrew, back in 1981, the worst mountaineering accident in American history occurred here on Rainier. On that tragic day, an avalanche swept 11 climbers to their death and sealed them in a crevasse on the Ingraham Glacier, right near where today's accident occurred."

"I know. I read about that in a book."

"But what you may not know is that Martin Graham, who at the time was one of the youngest professors at the University of Washington School of Medicine, was climbing alone high up on the mountain that day, directly above where the avalanche started. During the post-avalanche investigation, he told the rangers that he thought he caused the avalanche. He said that just prior to the avalanche, he fell but was able to self-arrest after a short slide. However, he said his slide knocked some snow and small ice chunks down a cliff, which then triggered the main avalanche below him."

"You're telling me Dr. Graham caused their deaths? That can't be true."

"There's more. Our rangers immediately went up the mountain to the spot where Graham slid, and they concluded that there was simply no way Graham's slide could have caused the main avalanche. His slide was too small. The sequential nature of the two was simply a coincidence. The official report concluded that a fluke of nature had caused the main avalanche, but Graham still blamed himself. Until today, the last news we had about Martin Graham was he left medical school and moved away. Now we know. The ghost of Rainier has closed another chapter in the history of this beautiful yet deadly mountain."

CHAPTER 31

Dr. Graham's death left me despondent and hopeless. Like Dr. Graham blaming himself for the death of the 11 climbers, I blamed myself for his death. If I hadn't asked him to train and climb with me, he'd still be alive. My own selfish pursuit had ended another man's life.

Shortly after the tragedy, friends and relatives gathered for a memorial service in Chicago. More than 500 people attended the serene event to share their memories and offer hope. I was surprised to see how many lives he had touched. The mayor of Chicago spoke, as did the head of the local hospital. Martin's brother shared some early memories of him, while about a hundred kids from the city sang a moving tribute. I also saw Tamara in the crowd. I didn't know how all these pieces fit together until midway through the service, Hank Kinnick approached the pulpit and spoke:

Every person matters. To Martin, it was as simple as that. Martin lived not for himself but for those around him who needed help. Having never married, his family knew no boundaries. Whether it was helping at the clinic he founded here in Chicago or traveling to his Brazilian clinic to help the helpless, Martin was always giving. He came to me many years ago to help him create a financial plan. His goal was clear—maximize the amount of money he could use to support the needs of those less fortunate than him. Usually, I teach people how to save. Martin taught me how to give.

The full room today is a testament to the fact that one person can make a difference. He comforted thousands, he saved hundreds, and he did it quietly. Well, almost. His passion for helping led him straight to city hall to be an advocate for the poor. It's good to see several people from city hall here today.

Death brings new life. Yes, today, we mourn Martin, but tomorrow we carry on his mission. What he started has no finish line. We simply pass the baton from Martin to the next person inspired to breathe new life into the lives of those in need.

In a cruel twist of fate, a tragic 1981 avalanche became the driving force behind Martin's burning desire to heal the sick and bring community to the inner city. Twenty years later, another avalanche ended his life. In between, he created a legacy by bringing people together and healing the hurting through his clinics. Out of tragedy, he found purpose, and he lived it. Some people will never find their purpose, content instead to let a life of broken dreams and hopeless regret slowly bury them until all their oxygen is gone. Others will seek and discover the purpose in their lives and make a lasting difference. Martin Graham made a lasting difference. Will you?

Hank's words left me gasping for air. It was as if he was speaking directly to me. *Slowly bury.* But through my grief, I couldn't hear him clearly.

CHAPTER 32

The guilt was overwhelming. I felt as though I'd killed Dr. Graham, and it was killing me. Sandra did the best she could by telling me that I didn't force him to go with me. He chose to go of his own free will, and what happened was an accident. Intellectually, I knew she was right, but emotionally, I still felt responsible.

With more than a hundred cable TV channels, Dr. Graham's death made the national news. The story was just too tempting to resist:

> Seattle medical school professor takes responsibility for causing avalanche death of 11 climbers in 1981. Disappears to Chicago and becomes country doctor. Opens clinics for the poor in inner-city Chicago and Brazil. Saves hundreds of lives. Climbs Rainier again after 20 years, and an avalanche entombs him on the mountain.

I turned down all requests for interviews; it was just too painful.

The resulting publicity made it difficult for me to show my face around town, so I retreated. I ran my business from home and let Colin take a lead role in running things. To my surprise, he did a great job of keeping the business afloat. He told me that my absence gave him the room to take responsibility and make things happen. I wondered what that said about my management style.

In the aftermath of the tragedy, I essentially disengaged from daily activity and retreated inward. I shut down from Sandra and the kids. I stopped working out with Tamara. Instead, I tried to get over Dr. Graham's death by "thinking" my way out of it. The loss also made me think about other losses in my life . . . my dad, my mom, not being connected to Sandra and the kids. I had regrets.

To help me avoid falling into an even deeper despair, Sandra suggested I start reading books again—anything to help pull me out of my despondency. Taking her advice, I researched some books online, then had Sandra pick them up for me at the bookstore and the library. I read about grieving and how you typically go through five stages: denial, anger, bargaining, depression, and acceptance. Another book talked about a three-stage grieving process, which included numbness, disorganization, and reorganization. I read Christian and Jewish books on death and dying. I read books about Buddhism and its take on death and life after death. I read books about the meaning of life. I read the great philosophers. I even read some self-help books to help achieve a more positive mental attitude. Ultimately, each book helped in some way, but it would take more than a book to pull me out of despair. It would take people.

CHAPTER 33

A few days after the memorial service, Hank called. He didn't call because he had a hot stock idea. He called because he wanted to talk.

Like me, Hank was grieving. Dr. Graham had been a client of his for almost 20 years, and they had worked closely on structuring Dr. Graham's finances so he could support the Chicago and Brazil clinics. Dr. Graham had not been just a client; he had also been a friend. Hank had been a wealth advisor for many years, and he'd had other clients who passed away. However, unlike most things in life, experience doesn't make death any easier.

I felt like a murderer who had escaped justice. Dr. Graham was dead, yet I was still alive and free to live my life. But living with the thought of what happened was like a life sentence without parole. Hank tried to set me straight.

"Guilt is a living death, and the way out is through forgiveness. Martin felt guilty for the death of those 11 climbers back in 1981, even though the rangers told him it was not his fault. Eventually, he realized that guilt, whether it was deserved or not, was preventing him from making something positive out of the tragedy. When he finally forgave himself and let go of the guilt, he was freed to build a legacy of help, healing, and hope for those less fortunate than him."

But no matter how much Hank and I talked about it, I still felt responsible for ending another man's life. Forgiveness wouldn't come easy.

Dr. Graham's death made me confront my own mortality. Maybe my obsessive pursuit of money and success was simply a misdirected way to try to avoid thinking about the inevitable cycle of life. I was scared that I might die to life before being buried for eternity.

"Death is a natural part of life, Andrew. We're born. We live. We die. It's those middle two words that seem to trip people up. Martin knew that a good life precedes a good death. Live a good life, and you'll never have to fear death. The best way to live a good life is to live each moment with love, gratitude, and compassion. Martin did that, and while his body died violently, his spirit continues to live peacefully."

I took some comfort in knowing that Martin's life, while artificially shortened, still made a difference. A huge difference actually. He had lived his calling, and the world was better for it.

When tragedy strikes, you tend to see the best and the worst in humanity. On the positive side, tragedy tends to reduce us all to the lowest common denominator. It strips away race, creed, and status, and reduces us all to the common denominator of our humanness. Sandra and Hank, as well as other people, were there for me, but it took me some time to shed the skin of my philosophy of rugged individualism and let them in.

Hank said, "We each grieve in our own way, yet in order to heal, we need to feel the connectedness of another human being. Healing is a sharing process." He was right.

Our conversations covered many different subjects, and at times, Hank challenged me. During one particularly telling conversation, he asked me a thoughtful question: "What do you think your family has wanted most from you?"

In hindsight, the answer was obvious, but in real time, it was not so easy to live because I'd let my career take priority. "They wanted me to be more engaged with them," I said with a twinge of regret. "Now that I look back on it, I can remember times when the kids were young and they'd ask me to play games with them, and I said I couldn't because I had to work. Eventually, they stopped asking." Ouch. I was really a schmuck.

To rationalize the trade-off, I'd made this deal with myself. Being a businessperson, I believed in the concept of division of labor. I did the work outside of the house, while Sandra took care of the work inside of the house. That meant I focused on my career and Sandra focused on the kids—and me. It had seemed like the efficient way to organize. I now saw the error of my ways.

Hank shared one final insight with me. He said that a healthy body could help heal a hurting mind. It seemed to work for him, because he was holding up better than I was. I was neglecting my workouts and reverting to my old bad eating habits.

I knew Hank was right about the exercising, but I was so busy feeling sorry for myself that I just let it slide. Sandra, in her wise way, didn't nag me to go back to the gym and start eating healthy again. She just did it herself, and her leading by example eventually led me back to my workouts with Tamara.

CHAPTER 34

I hadn't met with Tamara since before the accident, but when I called to set up an appointment, she was very happy to hear from me. We met a couple of days later and spent the first half hour sharing our grieving experience. Dr. Graham had been her inspiration and mentor for many years, and she was hurting, too. Eventually, our conversation turned to me, and she said we needed to take a new approach to my health. Instead of jumping right back into the weight lifting and cardio, she said we needed to work on my mental health.

"You're ready," she said.

"Ready for what?" I asked.

"To get serious about meditation."

"We've done the breathing exercise a few times. Isn't that enough?" I asked.

"It's not. Andrew, by quieting our mind through meditation, we can bring our mind, body, and spirit into a harmonious balance. Meditation allows us to peel away the layers of soot and emotional baggage that pollute our minds and prevent us from truly knowing ourselves."

While Tamara's comments bordered on the touchy-feely, I nodded with interest, and she kept talking.

"What I'm asking you to do, Andrew, is to take the time to slow down and connect with your authentic self. Please don't take this the wrong way, but from what you've told me, all your adult life, you've been chasing external things and trying to possess them. Even climbing the mountain, to some extent, was an act of possession, of trying to conquer the summit. When you meditate and go inward, you lose attachment to the things of life. Instead, you uncover what is already inside you—your true self with no mask. That's where you'll find your life's calling, your inner bliss."

"Okay, okay," I said. "I'm in. What do I need to do?"

Like a good coach, Tamara tested my commitment. "Andrew, I remember you said 'I'm in' before, yet your enthusiasm slipped, and you stopped working out. Are you for real this time?"

I couldn't let her down twice. "Yes, for real."

"I'm going to trust you on this, Andrew. For the next 40 days, I want you to meditate for a minimum of 15 minutes, preferably 30 minutes, each morning. Breathe, relax, let the serenity sink in. I want you to go to a place of peace. I want you to let go of the guilt, the hurt, and your past regrets. Find your faith and gain strength from it."

She made it sound so inviting, and I figured I had nothing to lose. I couldn't get much lower.

"I'll do it."

CHAPTER 35

On more than one occasion, I wondered why Sandra put up with me. I had definitely taken more from her than I had given in return. Her love really drove home the meaning of the words, "Till death do us part."

I didn't know what to expect from her when I came home to tell her about my new 40-day commitment to meditation.

"You know, honey, ever since the avalanche, I feel as though I was the one who was buried. I've been trying to figure out how to get out of the depression I'm in and find a new energy for you, the kids, and life in general. I met with Tamara today for the first time in a while, and she had a suggestion for me. She said I should get serious about meditating because it will help me shake some of the emotional baggage I'm carrying and lead me to my inner bliss. I want to be happy again, to feel joy, desire, hope."

"Really?" Sandra seemed surprised to hear the words *meditate* and *inner bliss* coming out of my mouth.

"Yes, really," I said with confidence.

"Well, I think that's a *really* good idea. This could be good for you," she said. With that, there was no turning back.

For the next 40 days, I began my day with a period of focused relaxation. Sitting in a chair with my hands in my lap, palms facing up, I meditated. I focused on my breath and let my thoughts move in and out of my mind.

I was skeptical about the benefits of this forced daily quiet time, yet after just the first few days, I noticed my energy level picking up and my outlook changing. Sandra and Tamara noticed, too, and they commented on how I seemed to be getting "better."

After 40 days, my daily sessions had become a ritual. It was something I looked forward to each morning, so I continued it. The benefits were building.

True to my businessperson form, I used several "strategies" to help pull me out of my emotional turmoil. I had occasional meetings with Hank for some male bonding. I worked out with Tamara to renew my body. And I meditated to bring balance to my mind, body, and spirit.

Feeling better, I decided it was time to live up to an earlier promise. I talked to Kellie and Kevin and told them I wanted to take each of them on a one-on-one trip. They could pick the place, and we'd do whatever they wanted. Their eyes lit up.

After thinking about it for a couple days, Kellie came back to me and said she knew where she wanted to go.

"I want to take a trip with you to Peoria, Dad."

"What's going on in Peoria, Illinois?"

"I want to drive down there with you and help build houses for Habitat for Humanity. I was reading on the Internet that they're looking for volunteers. They're doing a five-day blitz build, and I'd like to be a part of it."

I couldn't have been more proud of Kellie. I was expecting a shopping trip to New York or something like that. It showed how little I really knew her.

We left for Peoria about three weeks later and had a meaningful conversation during the three-hour drive.

"You know, Dad, you weren't around much when I was growing up, and for a long time, I harbored some resentment toward you. But now that I've been away at college for several years, I'm a little wiser, and I understand how life can be complicated and not always work out the way you want. I guess what I'm trying to say is, you're still my dad, and we've got lots of years ahead of us. Good years, I hope. Someday I'll have a family, and I want my kids to know their grandfather. You may not have always been there for me, but I want you to be there for them."

I reached for her hand and told her I was sorry. "I know I wasn't the best dad, but there's nothing I'd like more than to be the best grandpa."

The next five days were filled with the sound of pounding hammers, buzzing saws, and the hullabaloo of compassionate people working together to bring shelter to several grateful families. By the time we finished, our bodies were aching, but our spirits were soaring.

Kevin had a different idea about his one-on-one-trip with me.

"Let's go to Disney World," he said.

His choice also surprised me. He's a little old for that, I thought, but it was his trip, so he got to decide. We made that trip about a month after Kellie's trip.

During the flight from Chicago to Orlando, Kevin said he had a confession to make.

"Dad, I know you think it's a little strange that of all the places I could go, I chose Disney World. The reality is, it picked me."

"What do you mean?"

"When you asked me to go on a trip, I thought about all the people out there who are not as fortunate as I am. I have all I need, but other people don't. It got me thinking, so I talked to Mom, and she helped me contact the Make-A-Wish Foundation. We ended up connecting with Mr. Petrovick and his 11-year-old son Nathan, who has a degenerative muscular disease. Nathan badly wanted to go to Disney World, but his family couldn't afford it because of the medical bills. Mom said you wouldn't mind if we helped them make the trip, so we're meeting Nathan and his dad at the hotel later this evening. We'll spend a little time with them and help make their visit more enjoyable. I even got an Angel Flight pilot to transport them to Orlando."

My jaw dropped. Kellie and Kevin had grown up to be mature, compassionate kids who were now teaching me a lesson in life.

"And Dad, there's a second reason why I wanted to go to Disney World. When I was a kid, I wanted to go so badly, and you promised that you would take us there. For three years, you kept saying we'd go. But we never did. You were just too busy with work. I know how Nathan feels, and I didn't want him to miss out on what I missed."

I had to wipe the tears from my eyes as I said, "I'm sorry, Kevin. I'm sorry." It's all I could say.

After arriving at the Grand Floridian, two cast members kept us busy going over the resort and all the things we could do during our five-day stay. Just as they wrapped up, Mr. Petrovick and his son Nathan came in. After a big thank-you, we spent some time getting to know each other, and we mapped out our game plan.

Over the next few days, I watched the sheer joy on Nathan's face as he took in the sights and sounds of the park.

From the Disney characters wandering the park, to the fireworks shows, to a simple ice cream cone, Nathan absorbed and appreciated all of it. Being a small part of his dream come true was a hundred times better than any rush I'd ever gotten from cashing a bonus check.

Thanks to my kids, I participated in a slice of life that otherwise would have gone unnoticed.

Not long after the Disney World trip, Hank called just to touch base. Seizing an opportunity, I asked him if he would take me into the city and show me the clinic Dr. Graham founded. He was happy to do that, and we set a time for the following week.

It was a good thing Hank drove. He took me to a part of the city that I knew existed on a map but had never gone near. As we pulled into the parking lot, I was surprised at the size of the building. Turns out it was more than a clinic—it was a community center.

Inside, there was a medical clinic, a gym, a game room, a cafeteria, and several meeting rooms. We visited on a Monday afternoon and the place was full of activity. Kids were playing basketball, children were getting medical attention, the game room was hopping, and a couple of the meeting rooms were in session with what looked like some type of adult education. About 20 people were eating in the cafeteria.

Hank told me that Dr. Graham had been the catalyst for getting the facility built and that he had spent Mondays and Fridays there as well as part of the weekend. It then dawned on me that that's why he only worked Tuesday through Thursday at his other office. In a typical week, Hank said over 300 kids used the facility and dozens more were treated in the clinic. It was a similar story for the clinic Dr. Graham built in Sao Paulo, Brazil. He visited that one every six months for an extended stay.

Because Dr. Graham never married, he left his estate to the foundation he'd created to support these two clinics. Hank said that the life insurance proceeds swelled the coffers of the foundation, but the Chicago facility was frequently short on staff. After touring the facility and talking to some of the staff and the kids, I made a decision on the spot that I would come down each week and spend time helping out. Hank looked at me and said we could carpool. He had been helping at the facility since day one. No wonder everybody there knew his name.

My life was finally coming together in an uplifting and positive way. I was back at the office on a regular basis—without the overtime—and the business was going well. Colin was doing a fantastic job running the day-to-day activities, while I focused on sales and strategy. Helping at the clinic made me feel that I was making the world a little better place, and that was very gratifying. The wealth plan we had developed with Hank was performing as expected, so that was comforting. I was meeting with Tamara two to three times a week and continuing my daily meditation. As a father, I felt so much closer to the kids, particularly after the one-on-one trips. And Sandra and I were bonding in a way that had been absent for many years.

Still, 11 months after the avalanche, there was one piece missing.

CHAPTER 36

As I neared the one-year anniversary of the avalanche, I sat down with a notebook and began to write down my thoughts.

The darkest days of the immediate aftermath of the avalanche have passed. I can see clearly now. I'm in a good place with my conversations with Hank, my workouts with Tamara, and my meditation practice. Business is good. Sandra and I have rediscovered each other. The kids are incredible, and I'm being a much better father. I'm an avid reader and find pleasure in good books. All in all, things are pretty good. But . . . but what? I feel like something's still missing. Something's still gnawing at me and keeping me from fully moving forward with my life.

That evening, I lit two candles and opened a bottle of Sandra's favorite wine. I poured two glasses and held them in my hand.

"Sandra," I said. "We need to talk."

"Honey, what's wrong? Candles and wine—this isn't like you."

"I know. Here, let's make a toast. To my beautiful, understanding, and loving wife. No matter what happens, I love you and I always will."

"Andrew, you're scaring me. What's going on?"

"I have to tell you something."

"Tell me what?"

"I need you to trust me on this."

"Trust you on what? Tell me."

"I have to go back."

"Go back? Go back where?"

"To the mountain."

"Rainier? You've already done that. Why would you ever want to go back after all the pain it's caused?"

"Because I never said goodbye to Dr. Graham. It happened so fast. That's the one thing keeping me stuck in the past."

"Can't you say your goodbye from here?"

"No, I have to go back. I have to stand on the spot where it happened and feel the glacier under my feet."

"Oh, Andrew, I don't want you to go. You seemed to be doing much better, but now this. What happens if there's another avalanche? I couldn't bear to lose you over this."

"Don't worry. It's out of my hands. I *have* to go. The anniversary is next week, and I'm leaving on Tuesday."

CHAPTER 37

The feeling was much different the second time around. Rather than my naive enthusiasm from one year ago, I now felt an eerie sense of calm. I wasn't there to conquer the mountain, for no mountain can be conquered. I was there for an inner journey, to spend a night on the mountain alone with my thoughts and memories of that day one year ago, and see what I found . . . or uncovered.

I registered as a solo climber under an assumed name to avoid publicity. I checked into the Paradise Inn, which was situated at the foot of the mountain. It was built in 1917 out of massive timbers, and its huge lobby held opposing, two-story stone fireplaces. Its small sleeping rooms added to the charm. I felt very grounded and slept peacefully that evening.

In the morning, I woke up and did an extra long, prayer-filled meditation asking for strength and clarity. After a calorie-filled breakfast, I loaded up my backpack, strapped on my boots, grabbed my ski poles, and began the five-hour trek to Camp Muir.

No longer focused on conquering the summit, I absorbed the scenery around me. The first wildflowers of the summer were peeking out, adding a colorful carpet to the already magnificent skyline. The mountain basked in a white glow as the pristine winter snow still clung to its slopes.

As I hiked up the Muir snowfield, the hustle and bustle of life in Chicago began to ooze out of me, replaced by the mesmerizing sound of trampled snow under my feet. After pausing for a moment at about 8,000 feet, I closed my eyes and breathed deeply, making sure I was fully awake to my surroundings.

Further up, the crowds and the air got thinner while my mind grew clearer. Five hours after my start, I reached Camp Muir.

I staked my claim on one of the bunks and rested for a while. After a drink and a snack, I walked outside to look around. While gazing across the Cowlitz Glacier, somebody tapped me on my shoulder. I turned around slowly.

"Hello, Mr. Craver."

"Hello, Gator." My cover was blown but part of me felt relieved that he was here.

"It's been one year. I thought I might run into you here, so I made sure I was on duty this week," he said.

"Thanks. It's been a year of great change and growth in my life. I feel like I'm close to putting it behind me, but something inside me tugged at me to come back. I had to come back and say a final goodbye to Dr. Graham."

"That's common as people go through the grieving process. What are your plans?"

"I'm going to rest up here for a few hours, and then around midnight, I plan to climb to Ingraham Flats and spend the rest of the night there. After watching the sunrise, I'll make my way back down to Paradise and head home. Hopefully, this night on the mountain will be the last step in my recovery."

"Are you here alone?"

"Yes."

"You know the danger of this mountain. Why don't you rope up with me, and I'll lead you across the glacier and help you set up your tent."

"Thanks, but I need to do this alone."

"Mr. Craver, I've been rescuing people from this mountain for more than 15 years. I've seen the mountain at its best, and I've seen it at its hellish worst. Traveling alone, unroped, on the glaciers is just an invitation to disaster. I don't want you to become another statistic. I can't force you, but I ask you to reconsider my offer."

Gator was one of the best rangers in the park service, and his concern for the climbers was legendary. "Gator, I really do appreciate your concern, but I have to do this alone. I just have to." Being a man of the mountain, Gator understood. While shaking my hand, he said, "Be safe." Then he was off.

I walked a little farther and found a quiet spot to sit and take in the view. Looking to the south, I saw Mount Adams and Mount St. Helens peeking out of the clouds. As I surveyed the scene, an uneasy feeling came over me.

Maybe Gator was right. I'm not an experienced climber. I have no business climbing on glaciers in the middle of the night. This is crazy.

I started to breathe fast, and my heart began to race. But before I reached the panic stage, I remembered what Tamara taught me. I relaxed my body and closed my eyes. I focused on my breathing. Before long, I was back in control and visualizing how the rest of the evening would unfold. Calmly, I walked back to the hut and tried to get some rest.

Lying in the top bunk and staring at the ceiling, I couldn't fall asleep. I was okay with that, though. Over the past year, I had become comfortable with stillness.

At midnight, I got up and went through the ritual of eating, dressing, putting on my boots and crampons, and flipping on my headlamp. An hour later, I stepped outside to begin my climb. Then, from the light of my headlamp, I saw the outline of a solitary figure standing at the edge of the glacier, holding a rope. It was Gator. Like Sandra, he wasn't giving up on me.

At that moment, I realized that I *could* make this climb alone, but I didn't have to. He knew the pain I was going through and the closure I was seeking, and he was reaching out to me one more time. This time, I had the humility to accept.

With a silent understanding, we roped up and he led the way. I kept my head down and followed the well-defined path from Camp Muir to Ingraham Flats. About an hour later, I reached my destination—or so I thought.

Standing at Ingraham Flats, a feeling overtook me, and I involuntarily looked up the mountain. There it was, shrouded in darkness yet slightly visible in the reflection of the waning crescent moon—the jumbled mass of ice blocks where the avalanche had started. My body told me that's where I needed to spend the night.

I turned to Gator and said, "I know it's not the normal path but I need to go up there, up to the genesis of the avalanche."

Gator looked at me intently, testing my resolve. He could see that I wasn't about to back down.

"Follow me, I'll lead you up the Ingraham Direct route, but be careful. It's riddled with crevasses this time of year."

Veering off the normal path, we headed up the Ingraham Glacier instead of traversing it over to Disappointment Cleaver. I was now climbing by faith and not by sight. Slowly, I put one foot in front of the other, using the rest step to maintain my strength. My inner compass was guiding me, and I wasn't pushing myself up. Instead, something I couldn't explain was drawing me.

Suddenly, I broke through the snow. *Falling. Falling.* Instinctively, I jammed my ice axe into the snow ahead of me hoping I would hit ice and not a continuation of the crumbling snow bridge. It kept slipping and slicing through the snow as I fell farther into the crevasse. Just as I was about to give up hope, my rope became taut and I felt a tremendous jolt as if connected to a stiff bungee cord. Up above, Gator had arrested my fall.

Terribly shaken but unhurt, I dangled silently in the abyss with my headlamp illuminating my otherworldly surroundings, thinking how this was the final resting place of Dr. Graham. Within minutes, Gator had secured his position and helped me climb out.

"She's speaking to us," he said from his voice of experience.

Moving a safe distance from the crevasse, I stopped and reflected.

My ego nearly killed me. Had I not accepted Gator's offer to rope up with me, I could be dead now, irretrievably wedged at the bottom of a 100-foot crack in the ice. Instead, I learned a valuable lesson—I really do need other people.

Still panting heavily, I consciously took control of my breath and tried to calm myself. This mountain was not going to make it easy on me. Once I gathered myself, we started moving again. Slowly, I put one leg in front of the other for another 30 minutes, until large boulders of ice completely surrounded us. That was it; we couldn't climb any farther. We had just found our home for the night.

CHAPTER 38

Gator pitched a tent while I stood there, figuratively frozen in the moment.

"People come to the mountains for many reasons, Andrew. Some seek fun and camaraderie. Some come to challenge their physical limits and to feel alive. Some seek peace and understanding. Others look for forgiveness. Whatever you seek, Andrew, you will find. Whatever you ask for, you will receive."

As Gator ducked into the tent to rest, I decided to stay outside. I laid out my sleeping pad and partially zipped into my subzero sleeping bag. Rather than trying to sleep, I sat upright with my back against a large block of ice. It was like camping under the stars with one minor exception—I was nearly 12,000 feet up on the most heavily glaciated mountain in the continental United States, dwarfed by blocks of ice as tall as two-story buildings.

Far below, I could see the faint glow from the other climbers' headlamps as they made their way across the Ingraham Glacier toward Disappointment Cleaver. Above I could see the stars, so close they looked like glowing white pumpkins mysteriously suspended in a black ether.

Wanting to absorb this moment and be fully alive to my environment, I consciously relaxed my body and slowed my breath. Gradually, as I became more relaxed, I became keenly aware of the sounds around me.

I could hear the wind as it swirled around the unbending frozen edifices. I could hear the creaking of the slowly moving mountain of ice beneath me as it inexorably inched its way down the mountain. I could hear the sound of my own thoughts.

In my head, I replayed the scene from one year ago over and over again.

What could I have done differently? Was it my fault? Why did it happen? What does it mean?

No matter how many times I replayed it, the result was still the same. Death.

I unzipped a pocket on my backpack and pulled out the original letter from Dr. Graham, the one he gave me before the aerial meeting. Illuminating it with the focused beam of my headlamp, I began to understand what Dr. Graham was trying to teach me.

> Be a living example of . . .
> Stick to . . .
> Be driven by . . .
> Be accountable through . . .
> Cherish your . . .
> Value your . . .
> Wisely use your . . .
> Find ways to . . .
> Be open to . . .

His role as teacher was to ask the right questions. My role as student was to find the right answers.

I had to discover the answers for myself, using guidance from other people such as Hank, Tamara, Edwin, Colin,

Gator, Sandra, and Kellie and Kevin. My teachers were all around me; it had just taken me a while to realize it.

As I put the letter down, my mind began to wander, and I thought about my life, my family, and my beliefs.

What was important to me? What was the meaning of my life? What was I put here to do? How can I make a difference?

Time began to bend as minutes became hours, hours became seconds. Eyes opened or closed—it didn't matter. My perception was morphing into its own consciousness, and my mind filled with evanescent glimpses of the extraordinary.

The temperature continued to drop, but I was basking in the warmth of my personal vision, a vision of life that transcended mere marginal existence. My eyes opened to the possibilities, my soul uncovered the wisdom of the ages locked inside of me, and my hand dutifully recorded it.

Slowly and beautifully, the arc of the southeastern sky began to radiate an intense palette of artistic color from the rays of the rising sun. Washington was awakening to a new day, and I to a new life.

With a renewed sense of being, I packed up with Gator and began down climbing. However, before I left the mountain, I needed to make one more stop. Gator led as we made our way down the boulder-strewn glacial expanse until we came to the chasm in the ice, the vortex that continues to hold its grip on the body of Dr. Graham. Gator gave me some space as I sat down near the edge and peered into the tomb.

The resplendence of the deep blue walls betrayed the death within them.

Peace washed over me. I felt his presence. I felt connected to him in the way that we are all connected to one another. Connected in the way that not even death can take away.

Looking up, I prayed. I prayed that Dr. Graham had found eternal peace. I prayed that his death would bring new life. I prayed for forgiveness. I prayed for strength and resoluteness of purpose. Then I said goodbye.

Closure, at last.

CHAPTER 39

As I made the final few slushy footprints that marked the end of my trek down the mountain that afternoon, there was a noticeable spring in my step; a lightness I hadn't felt before. The weight of years of accumulated mental muck was gone, sloughed away like the avalanche. I turned and took one more look at the horizon-filling white orb with its jagged ridges, its jigsaw maze of frozen blocks, and its masterful silhouette against the rich blue sky . . . and smiled. I smiled from the deepest part of my being and knew what was once buried was now uncovered.

In a bow to modern civilization, I pulled out my cell phone and called Sandra on her cell to let her know I was alive—and smiling. She was ecstatic and ended the call by saying, "I love you. We'll see you very soon."

I walked into the Paradise Inn and bought a sports drink to help replenish the fluids I'd lost over the past couple of days. I made my way back into the breathtaking lobby and started drinking while admiring the stone fireplaces and the peeled-wood beams. Just then, several voices in unison cried out, "Surprise!"

Before I knew what was going on, Sandra, Kellie, and Kevin had smothered me in a Craver family sandwich. I felt the love envelop me as we all coalesced into one being right there in the middle of the Paradise Inn lobby.

It was exhilarating to be back with the family, back in a way we'd never been before. I had so much to share with them, and now was the perfect time. After cleaning up and sharing a meal, we headed outside and built a roaring campfire in the shadow of the majestic mountain.

We roasted marshmallows and made s'mores while singing campfire songs—just like in the old days. There was enough joy and loving spirit around that campfire to fill a football stadium. Finally, I decided it was time. I threw a couple more logs on the fire and gathered everybody close. It was time to share my journey. After taking a deep breath, I began:

Sandra, my soul mate, Kellie and Kevin, the two greatest kids a dad could ever hope for, I'm sorry. I'm sorry I was such a schmuck for so many years, but that is in the past and we can't change it. Now and going forward is what we can affect, and that is exactly what I'm going to do. I've grown more in the last couple of years than the previous 43 combined. I know, some people are slow learners, and I'm one of them . . . but at least I learned!

Life is an odyssey for each of us, and along the way, we learn how to live, we learn how to be alive to life, and we learn how to die. My odyssey is not the same as yours, but the lessons are universal. These lessons lead to what we are all after in life—True Wealth. True Wealth is what money can't buy and death can't take away.

Up on that mountain, I didn't discover the secret to a life filled with true wealth—I uncovered it. You see, each of us is born with a wisdom that transcends time. Each of us has the seeds of greatness lying within us, and all it takes is two things to make those seeds grow. We need storms to blow in and bring rain to water those seeds, and we need sunshine to stoke the seeds' growth. I've had both. We all have both at one time or another.

None of us goes through life unscathed. Storms happen, and when they do, we need to use them as experiences to learn from and to grow. Always remember that the sun will eventually shine again, as it has for me.

I'm sorry I confused having money with having wealth. Dr. Graham, Hank, Tamara, Edwin, and the three of you helped point me toward the path to True Wealth over the past couple of years. Now I've pulled it all together, and I'm so excited to share it with you. Here's what I've learned:

1. ***Be a living example of the transformational power of love.***
   I know that Sandra's unconditional love has transformed me from a self-centered clod to a family-centered man who deeply loves each of you. You all mean the world to me.

2. ***Stick to your core values.*** *For many years, I was driven by money, and in some respects, it was my god. I worshipped at the altar of greenbacks, but at what cost? Eventually, decision day arrived with Edwin Luther's lakefront development, and I had to choose between going for the cash or going for what was true and right. Once that barrier was broken, I was able to start a journey that helped me reprioritize my life and uncover and live by what was truly important.*

3. ***Be driven by your purpose.*** *When we're born, our purpose in life is quite simple. We want food, clothing, shelter, and a clean diaper. But as we grow, so does our purpose. I believe we are all here for a reason, and the sooner we can figure out that*

reason, the better. Find the intersection of what you love to do and where you can make a difference, and you will find your purpose. My purpose, which I see with great clarity now, is to enhance the environment and to encourage and inspire other people to find True Wealth in their lives.

4. **Be accountable through your goals.** *Goals challenge us. They stretch us to think bigger and try harder than we would without them. They help us measure our progress through life. When set for the right reasons, goals motivate us to take action when we're tired, to dream big when we're feeling small, and to persevere when we're facing obstacles.*

5. **Cherish your relationships.** *Nothing in life is more enriching than having close, genuine relationships with those you love. Relationships are not easy. They require attention, commitment, and a sincere desire to be close to another human being. Miss out on true heartfelt relationships, and you will miss out on life itself.*

6. **Value your health.** *With so much to live for, there is no reason to die prematurely through unhealthy habits. Replenish your body with foods that nourish it. Do aerobic exercises to maximize the efficiency of your cardiovascular system. Lift weights to raise your metabolism and strengthen your body. Make conscious relaxation a part of your day.*

7. **Wisely use your financial resources.** *Financial success should be a by-product of doing everything else in our lives the right way. Money is not the goal; it's the result of doing the right things, at the right time, on purpose. Live well but not greedily.*

> *When you are financially successful, become a conduit to do even greater things for your place of worship, your community, and society.*

8. **Find ways to be compassionate with the world.** *There will always be people less fortunate than you. The greatest gift you can give is to help another person in need, so when you see pain and suffering, alleviate it. As St. Francis said, where you see despair, bring hope; where you see darkness, bring light; where you see sadness, bring joy.*

9. **Be open to wise counselors.** *Seek the advice of financial professionals who can steer you onto a path of personal and financial freedom. Seek the advice of fitness experts who can help you live a healthy life. Seek the advice of other teachers, coaches, and professionals whose messages connect and resonate with you. However, always remember that you are your best teacher. No matter what you hear or read, make sure it is congruent with your values, your purpose, and your faith.*

> *If you incorporate these nine universal principles into your life, True Wealth will be yours—almost. Yes, there is one more key: We each must have the capacity to forgive those who hurt us and to forgive ourselves when we cause the pain. Anger and bitterness are destructive emotions that destroy life—our life and others'. I have forgiven my father for his absence, and I hope you will forgive me for mine.*

When I finished my discourse, I found myself in my second Craver family sandwich of the day, and there wasn't a dry eye in the pack. In our group hug, time began to bend again as minutes became hours, and hours became seconds. By the time we came to, the campfire had mysteriously started roaring again as it drew energy from our love.

Sandra stood up as the heartwarming flame of the campfire accentuated the beatific glow on her soft, golden face. She looked at me and smiled, and said, "Welcome home, my love."

EPILOGUE

Five Years Later

"Andrew, would you please stop pacing—you're making me nervous," said Sandra.

I couldn't help it. I was about to become a grandpa. Kellie and her husband, Clay, were within minutes of blessing us with a miracle of new life.

Trying to remain calm, I took a moment to reflect on the past few years.

Since I stepped off the mountain five years ago, so much has changed. My relationship with Sandra is deep and meaningful. Kellie and Kevin live nearby, and we get together frequently and immensely enjoy our time together. Everybody's healthy. Thanks to Hank, I haven't had to worry at all about our financial situation. And our little franchise is not so little anymore. Once I got my priorities straight and stopped focusing on trying to make a ton of money, I ended up making more money than ever—and so did Colin. Dr. Graham's clinics and our charitable foundation have been the beneficiaries of our financial prosperity. Even my speaking business is going well, and audiences around the country are warming up to my message of getting on the path to True Wealth.

It certainly wasn't easy getting here, but the journey was well worth it. And we're not finished yet!

"Mr. and Mrs. Craver, Kevin, you can come in now. Your daughter has some good news."

On our brisk walk to the birthing room, the nurse told us that Kellie was doing great and the delivery was just perfect. As we opened the door, Kellie and Clay were cradling their little baby and beaming.

"Mom, Dad, meet your new grandson."

I just melted seeing the new addition to our family.

"Kellie and Clay, I'm so happy for you. A child is such a gift, congratulations."

"Dad, I want you to hold him." I picked him up, and Sandra and I just looked at him with his rosy face and tiny features. "Do you remember years ago, Dad, when I said I want my kids to know their grandfather?" asked Kellie.

"Yes, I do remember that. We were driving down to Peoria to build some houses, and I said I'd like nothing more than to be the best grandpa ever."

"Well, I really meant what I said, and I hope you did, too. He's a part of you, and we named him after you. His name is Andrew Nicholas Potter.

My emotions got the best of me. I lost it. At 50 years of age, my daughter was giving me a second chance to be a great parent, in this case, a grandparent. Miracles do happen.

ABOUT THIS BOOK

Our hope is that *Avalanche* will inspire you to find your own path to True Wealth. We give you the map and a compass and can help guide you, but ultimately, you need to find what True Wealth means to you. To help fulfill our mission, we created the website *www.truewealthcommunity.com* as a place for people to find the latest information about pursuing a life of True Wealth. Please visit the site and share it with your friends.

When you are ready to take the next step on your path to True Wealth, here are some suggestions.

- Highlight the sections in the book that really connected with you so you can refer easily to them in the future.
- Visit *www.truewealthcommunity.com* and explore the additional tools available to you.
- Download and complete the Blueprinting Exercises. Take your time and make doing them meaningful. Refer back to the sections in the book that you highlighted as you seek deeper understanding.
- Follow the nine principles for uncovering True Wealth.

- And most importantly, be a living example of the transformational power of love.

We would love to hear your feedback on the book. How did it affect you? Which part did you connect with the most? What changes have you made in your life? Are you on the path to True Wealth? Please let us know. You can reach us at *feedback@truewealthcommunity.com.* If you know someone who could benefit from reading the book, please share it with that person, too. Your kindness could be exactly what they need at that moment.

Together, we can all make this world a better place.

Steve Sanduski
Ron Carson

STEVE'S ACKNOWLEDGMENTS

As we move through life, we become wiser and I've been fortunate to have some great teachers along the way. I want to begin by thanking my wife, Linda. It's scary to envision the person I would be today if you had not come into my life. You've opened my eyes to so much more than I can ever repay. From the early, carefree days of the 1980s to the family-filled days of today, having you in my life along each step of the way is truly a blessing. I love you.

My daughters—Paige, Cori, and Tenley—how did I get so lucky? Each of you are so special, and even though I'm your dad, you still teach me a few lessons. It is a true joy watching you grow, mature, and make your way in the world. I love you.

There are two people in my life who have been there since day one. Mom and Dad, thank you for your love, your understanding, and your unwavering support all these years. I probably made you prematurely gray, but I hope I'm making up for it now. I love you.

My brothers Jim and Tom, my sister Mary, and your families, while we may live far apart, you're never far apart in my heart. I love you.

To Walt and Joy Anderson, you've treated me like a son for more than 20 years, and I can't thank you enough. I know where Linda gets her wonderful qualities. I love you.

To Kevin and Kathy, Joe and Joyce, John and Mari, John and Cindy, Scott and Diane, Tim, and my college roommate Mike, thanks for the great memories and your friendship. I also want to thank Pastor Ken Wittrock, Pastor Brad Meyer, and Cheryl Griess for your meaningful messages and all your support over the years. Linda and I have been blessed to have all of you in our lives.

Two people deserve special recognition for providing me with the invaluable feedback that helped improve the book and hone its message. Linda, you read countless drafts, and your keen insights are sprinkled throughout. Shannon Berning, acquisitions editor at Kaplan, you've been a true pleasure to work with, and your feedback and editing have been excellent—thank you.

I also want to thank my athletic coaches—Skip Morris, Beanie Lawrence, and John Coughlin—each of whom helped instill in me the value of hard work, teamwork, and sportsmanship. In recent years, as I added strength training to my workouts, personal trainer and all-around great guy Tom Roth has been influential in my thinking about health. And thanks again for the cameo appearance at Linda's 40th birthday party! We still talk about it. Todd Mills and the staff at Better Bodies, thank you for running a great fitness facility.

Mountain rangers, climbing guides, and expert rescue volunteers have saved countless lives through their dedication and selflessness, and they all deserve a huge thank-you. In particular, I want to recognize and thank Mike Gauthier, lead climbing ranger at Mount Rainier National Park.

Ron Carson, as my partner at PEAK, I thank you for your wise counsel, your energy, and your passion for helping other people. I have learned a great deal from you. What we're building at PEAK and through this book is part of my path to True Wealth.

I want to thank the incredibly dedicated team at PEAK for your loyalty and your desire to help people. You make every day a learning experience for me, and the impact you're having on our clients is life changing.

Finally, a special thanks to all of our clients at PEAK. It is a privilege to work with you and to learn from you. Together we can help people get on the path to True Wealth.

RON'S ACKNOWLEDGMENTS ∎

There are so many people that I want to acknowledge for my personal and professional success. Starting with my younger years, there's my parents. First, my mom, who brought me into the world and to this day still nurtures me. She's my absolute number one biggest fan. I've never had any bigger supporter than her. Mom, I'll always remember all of the things you've done and continue to do for me. To my father, who has tremendous drive and unbelievable work ethic, you have blessed me with these. I work hard from your example, and I'm not afraid to try things, or to fail, as long as I learn from them. From that, I draw a tremendous amount of my burning desire to succeed. Next, my sister. You're one of my biggest supporters and also very encouraging. I love and appreciate all you do.

Through my junior high and high school years, coaches Hunt and Gentzler were two of my early mentors who gave me tremendous confidence when I was young and impressionable. Coach Gentzler, my junior high coach, was a great teacher, very gentle but firm. He was able to push when I needed it and also console and give fatherly advice when needed. Coach Hunt, my football coach, was a good friend and tremendous teacher. Coach Hunt, I still have the note that you sent home when I earned 100 percent on my civics test. You told me that I could achieve anything, and I believed it. Thank you. You were tough but perfect. I'll always remember all you've done for me. Through my younger years, there was also my Uncle Dale. Dale, when I was a little boy, you'd take me to play sports. I remember your taking me to buy a baseball glove and to Nebraska football games. You have a tremendous amount to do with my love and interest in sports.

Now to my high school sweetheart, wife, and the love of my life, Jeanie: you've been there from the beginning and supported me in every way. You're my biggest cheerleader. I love you so much! I love everything that you've done and continue to do for me. I couldn't have begun to have the success that I have without your tremendous involvement and support in my life. To our three beautiful children, Chelsie, Maddy, and Grant: you truly have given me meaning and purpose in my life. There is no greater accomplishment that I'll ever have than seeing you progress through the world and have you live a life as full of meaning and purpose as I have and you have given me. Thank you, and I love you all to eternity plus one!

I also want to thank Jim Putnam. Early on when I had success in my career, you were there to give me guidance and counsel and put things in perspective for me. To my dear friend, Jason Comes: it seems like yesterday that we were in the fourth grade together. Then we became college roommates, and the next thing, you were serving as best man in my wedding. I love you like a brother.

To my Carson Wealth Management Group team, you are absolutely the best wealth management team in the country. We're constantly ranked in the top five nationally, and you never take that for granted. You seem to be pleased with our success but never satisfied, always wanting to improve and take it to the next level. You're truly a unique group of individuals. Thank you for being there for me.

To the PEAK team: wow, unbelievable! We have built the country's premier coaching and software organization for financial advisors. You've done this by giving 100 percent of your soul, each and every day, to make PEAK the best company it can be. I look forward to working with you every day and having all of you on my team. I could not have had any of the business success without your efforts.

To Steve Sanduski, my partner in PEAK: I couldn't have done this book without you. Obviously, you did all the heavy lifting. While we collaborated on the ideas for the book, you turned them into a masterpiece on paper. You clearly have a great gift, and for that I want to thank you.

Finally, I hope all of you enjoy the book. I know that you will recognize some of the events and sayings, as part of what happens in the book comes from my own and my clients' lives over the years. I hope that you can build your True Wealth as a result of this book.

ABOUT THE AUTHORS

Steve Sanduski, MBA, CFP®, is a writer, speaker, and businessman who has helped build three multimillion dollar businesses. As the managing partner of PEAK, a financial advisor coaching, software, and consulting company, Steve was the cocreator of the Quest for Excellence™ national coaching program and the PEAK Academy™.

In the 1990s, Steve was one of the three initial employees of a start-up registered investment advisory firm and he helped the firm raise over $1.5 billion in five years. From there, he became president of a start-up broker-dealer and ushered it through its early growth phase. At that firm, Steve helped foster the concept of collaborative wealth planning by teaming financial advisors, estate planning attorneys, and CPAs to provide comprehensive wealth planning to individuals with complex needs. Since 1993, he has delivered keynote presentations to thousands of advisors and investors throughout the country.

In the 1980s, he worked for three blue-chip companies, Caterpillar, Hewlett-Packard, and First Data Corporation, in a variety of financial management roles.

An experienced writer, Steve is the coauthor of *Tested in the Trenches* (Kaplan, 2005). He also writes articles on life planning, personal development, investing, and practice management for trade magazines, broker-dealer publications, and the general public. In 2006–2007, he was a community columnist for the *Milwaukee Journal Sentinel.*

Steve received a bachelor's degree in finance from Illinois State University and a master's degree in business administration from Indiana University. He is also a Certified Financial Planner™ and previously held the NASD Series 7, 24, 63, and 65 licenses.

Steve and his wife Linda have three beautiful daughters. He enjoys family and friends, traveling, reading, early morning bike rides, and being anywhere near water and mountains—particularly Mount Rainier—which kindly allowed him to summit (without any major drama) in 2004.

Ron Carson, CFP®, CFS, ChFC, is president of Carson Wealth Management Group, a comprehensive wealth planning firm, and founder of PEAK, a coaching, software, and consulting company.

With over 20 years of experience and more than $1 billion in invested assets, Ron is one of the country's most successful and respected financial advisors. His average client has a net worth of more than $10 million and has an account minimum of $5 million. Most recently, *Registered Rep* listed Ron as one of the "Top 50 Financial Advisors" within the investment industry as a whole. For five years, he was selected by *Worth* magazine as one of the "Best 200 Financial Advisors" in the country. J.K. Lasser selected him as one of the "Nation's Top Financial Advisors." For three years, *Medical Economics* selected him as one of the "Nation's Top 150 Wealth Advisors."

As a former guest on CNBC's *Power Lunch* and as the former host of the business segment on the CBS affiliate KMTV three days per week, Ron has become well-known locally and nationally. For 13 years, Ron was the cohost of the nationally syndicated weekly radio show *Financial Focus,* broadcast on over 100 stations around the country.

Ron's other accomplishments include the following:

- Ranked the number one representative for more than 16 consecutive years at LPL Financial Services, the nation's largest independent broker-dealer with over 9,000 representatives
- Ranked the number one independent rep out of 70,000, according to *Registered Rep* magazine
- Ranked the number one independent team in the *Winner's Circle* book and ranked the highest individual independent rep
- Ranked in *Barron's* "Top 100 Wealth Advisors"
- Founder of the American Charitable Foundation, which works for a more efficient disposition of charitable assets
- Past president of the Child Saving Institute
- Cofounder of the Heartland Chapter of the International Association of Financial Planning (now known as the Financial Planning Association)

In addition to his planning practice, Ron is recognized as one of the country's top trainers for financial advisors. He has spoken on five continents to groups as large as 3,000. Through keynote presentations, the Quest for Excellence™ national coaching program, and the PEAK Academy™, he teaches financial advisors his Tested in the Trenches™ ideas to help them develop their practices and enhance their quality of life. Additionally, PEAK's Breaking Away™ software is considered among its users to be the number one client relationship management software for financial advisors.

Ron's academic credentials include being a Certified Financial Planner™ practitioner, Certified Fund Specialist, and a Chartered Financial Consultant. He holds the NASD Series 7, 24, 63, and 65 licenses. Ron and his wife Jeanie have three wonderful children, and he enjoys golfing, flying, and entertaining family and friends.